THE WORLD
ACCORDING TO
HE & SHE

THE WORLD ACCORDING TO
HE & SHE

Julie Logan and
Arthur Howard

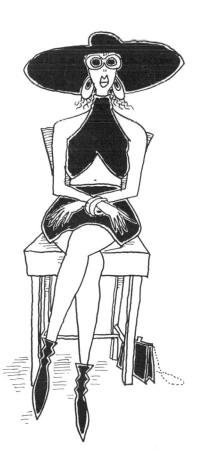

A Dell Trade Paperback

A DELL TRADE PAPERBACK

Published by
Dell Publishing
a division of
Bantam Doubleday Dell Publishing Group, Inc.
666 Fifth Avenue
New York, New York 10103

Excerpts from Sigmund Freud (p. 70)

Lecture XX
"The Sexual Life of Human Beings"
Introductory Lectures on Psychoanalysis
(1916–17 [1915–1917])

Lecture XXXIII
"Femininity"
New Introductory Lectures on Psychoanalysis 1933

ISBN: 0-440-50378-7

Printed in the United States of America

Published simultaneously in Canada

Book design by Robin Arzt

February 1992

10 9 8 7 6 5 4 3 2 1

RRH

ACKNOWLEDGMENTS

From both of us. Our heartfelt thanks to our editor, Jody Rein, for her enthusiasm and encouragement. Many more of the same to our agent, Loretta Fidel, for her cheerleading and support all along. And thank you, too, to Robin Arzt for bringing this across the finish line.

From Julie Logan. A multitude of gratitude to Roberto of Roark Graphic Supplies, Danny Justman and Rae Grieco of Typesetting, Ink, and Mort Cousens, Russ Weis, and Paul Flores at Copyrite Printers for their help in the initial stages of this project. For valued insights and moral support *in medias res* (and in no particular order), there are smartypants Jennie Nash, saucy Suzanne Munchower, savvy Steve Sager, supreme Colleen Wootton, ingenious Greg Glenn, near-genius Lucia Ludovico, no-jive John Newsom, stylin' Gina DeDomenico, laugh-riot Rita Hinkley, beatmeister Jon Valen (for the record), lovely Julie Platus, snappy Cinnia Curran, megatalented Phil Roberts, sterling Linda Dozoretz, soul of grace Carol Walker, heroic Peter Stern, oh-so fine Frank Voci and that Bob guy David Rensin. Many thanks, too, to Mary Peacock, who helped hatch the idea a long time ago and to Matt Groening at the beginning of everything.

From Arthur Howard. Thank you Luisa, Ted, and Jim.

CONTENTS

"Nobody understands the boy-girl stuff. . . .
Not even God."

—RALPH LOMBREGLIA

— CHAPTER I —

MATING RITUALS

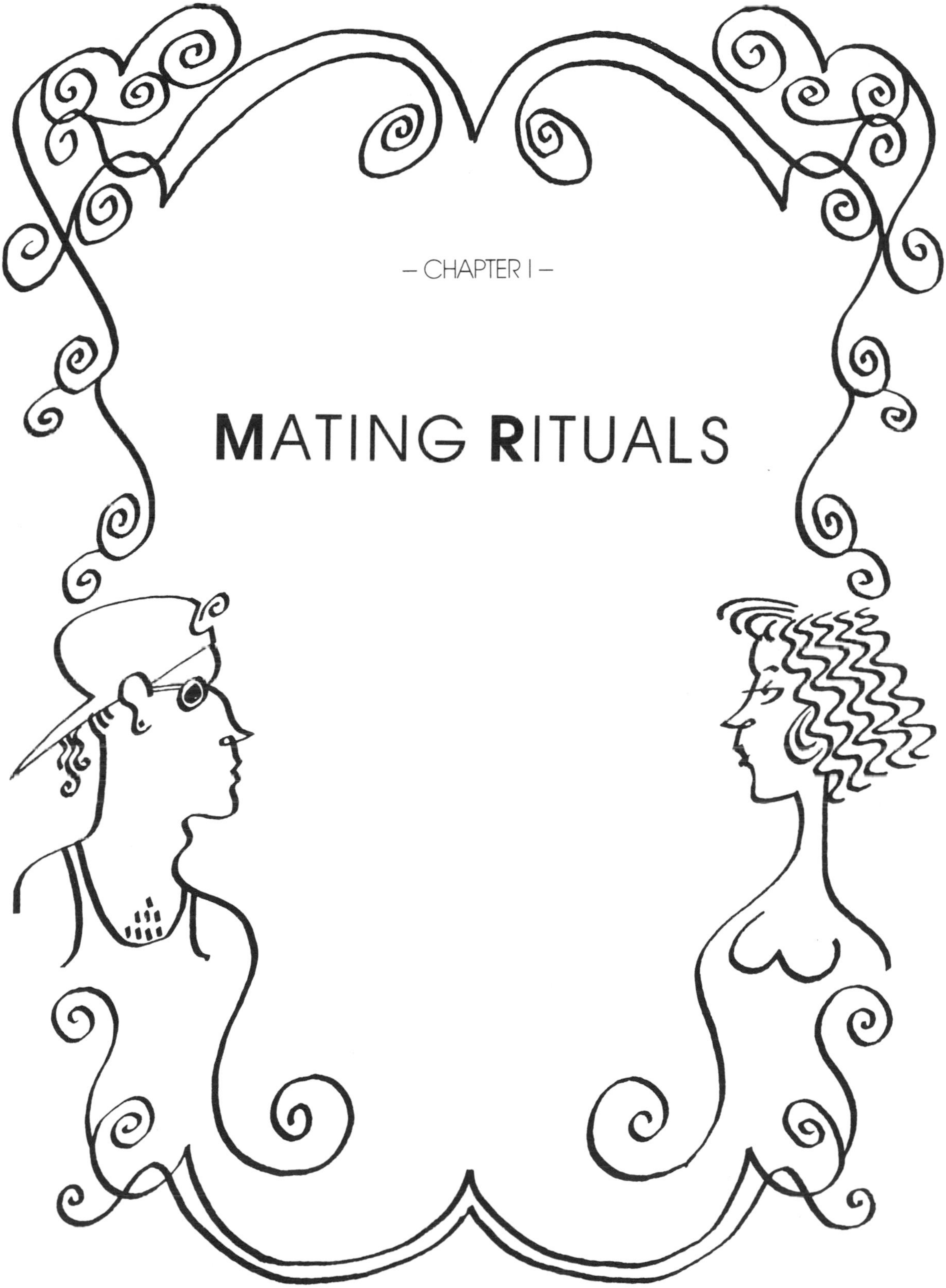

THE FIRST GLANCE

SHE

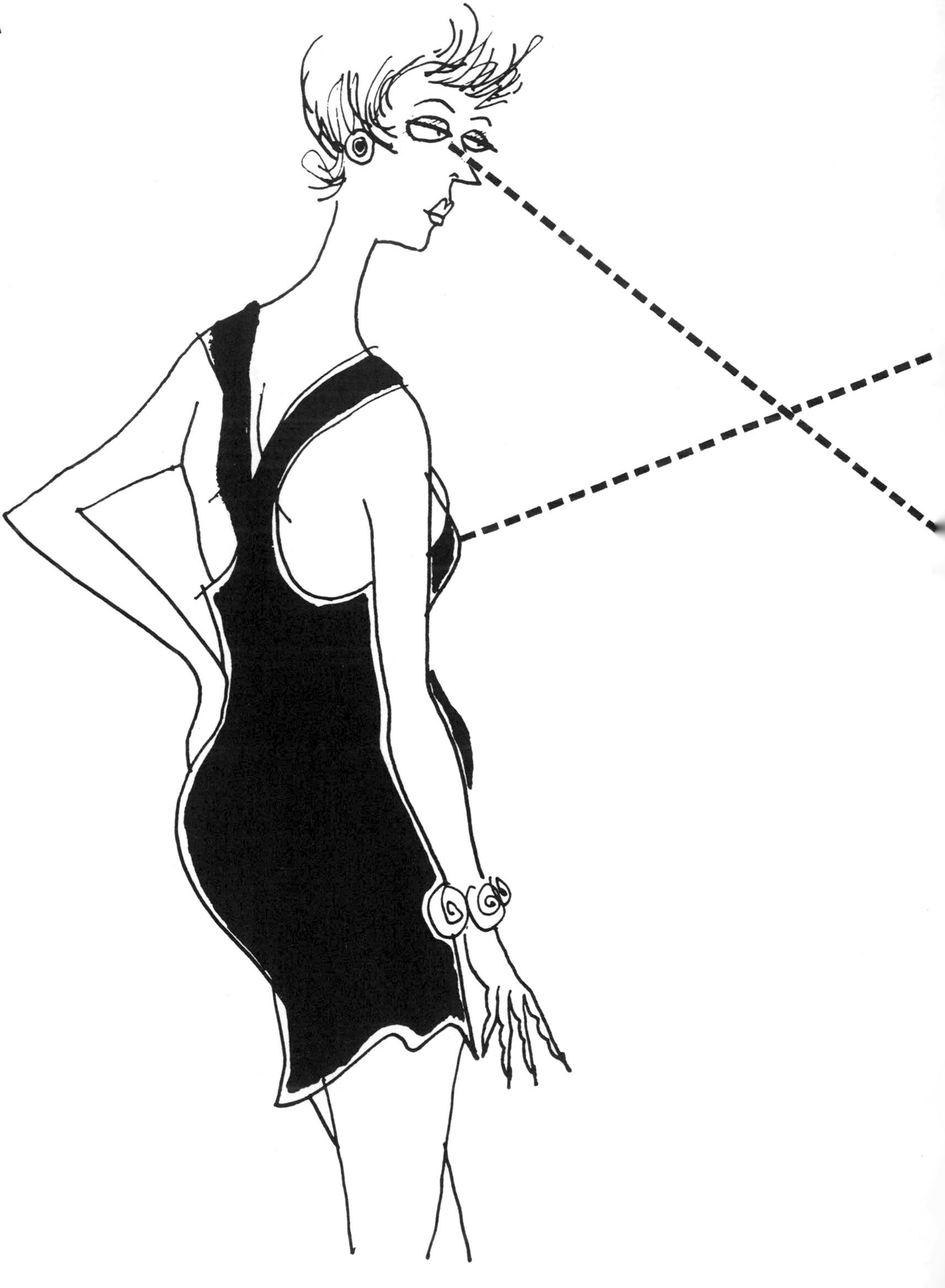

HE

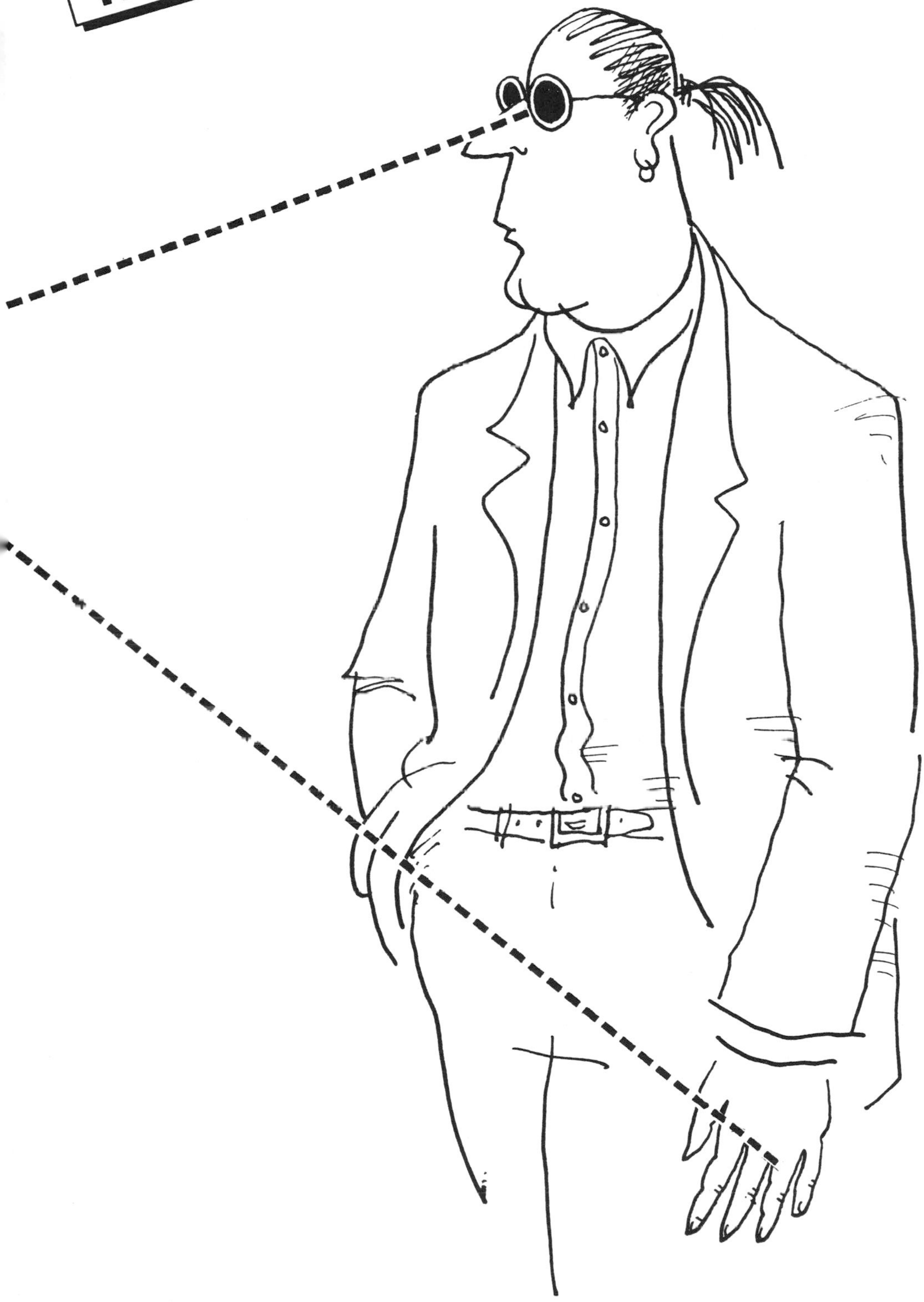

COUNTDOWN TO DATE NIGHT

SHE

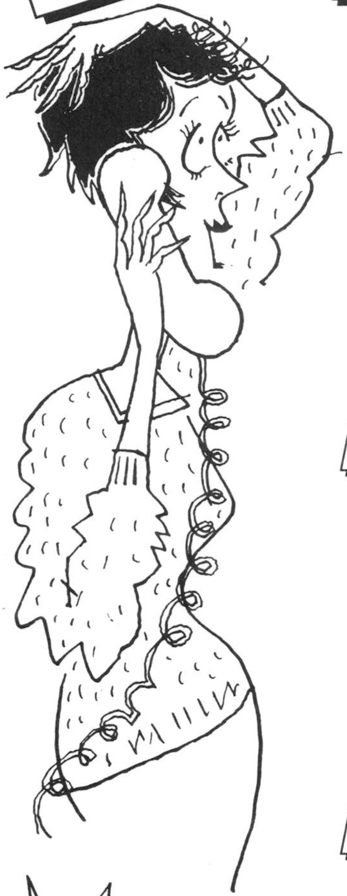

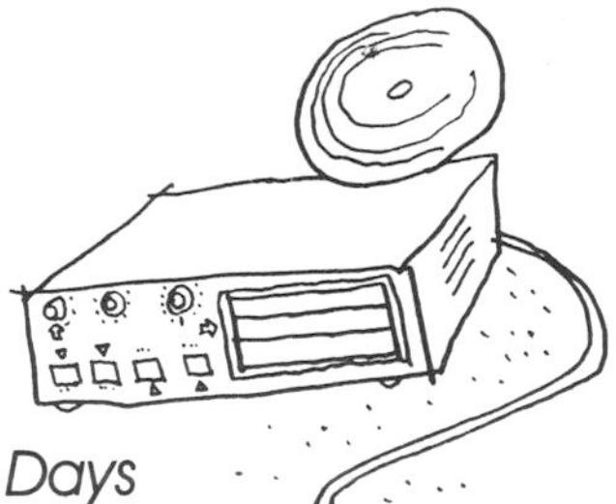

Tuesday

Calls best friend
Makes beauty appointments
Shoe repair
Narrows wardrobe choices
down to 3
Scores copy of *Thin Thighs in 30 Days*
Starts 3-day cleansing fast
Leg lifts (65 each side), 20 sit-ups,
45 butt tucks

Wednesday

Buys CD player and new tunes
Teeth cleaned at dentist
65 leg lifts, 35 sit-ups, 55 butt tucks
Tries on all 3 outfits, all are unsuitable.
Despair
Calls best friend
Refinishes coffee table

Thursday

Meets best friend at lunch for serious
shopping
Surrenders to strapless sarong (looks
great in the dressing room)
New underwear, perfume, candles
75 leg lifts, sit-ups, and butt
tucks
Mends kimono
Takes diuretic

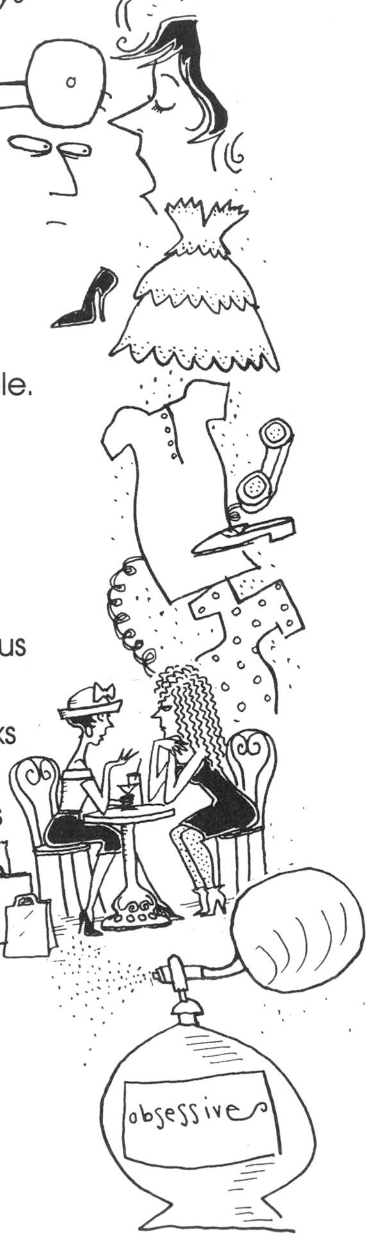
obsessive

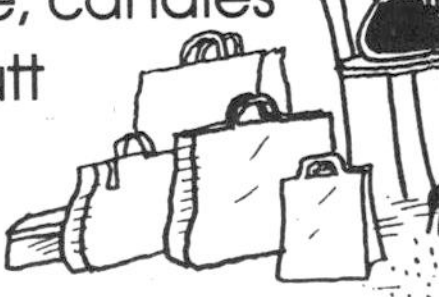

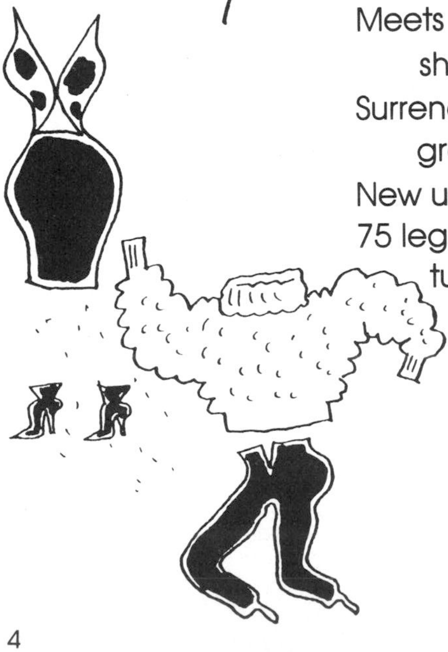

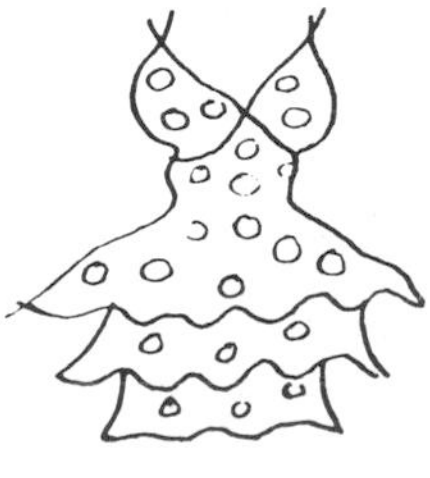

Friday

Calls in sick to work
Sauna, massage, bikini wax, cellulite
    mud wrap, deep pore cleansing,
    manicure, pedicure, lash tint, haircut, and blow-dry
Buys hosiery, Binaca, Breath Savers, and condoms
7 butt tucks (losing heart but working deep)
Gets dimmer switch installed
Sleeps 8 hours to awaken fully refreshed

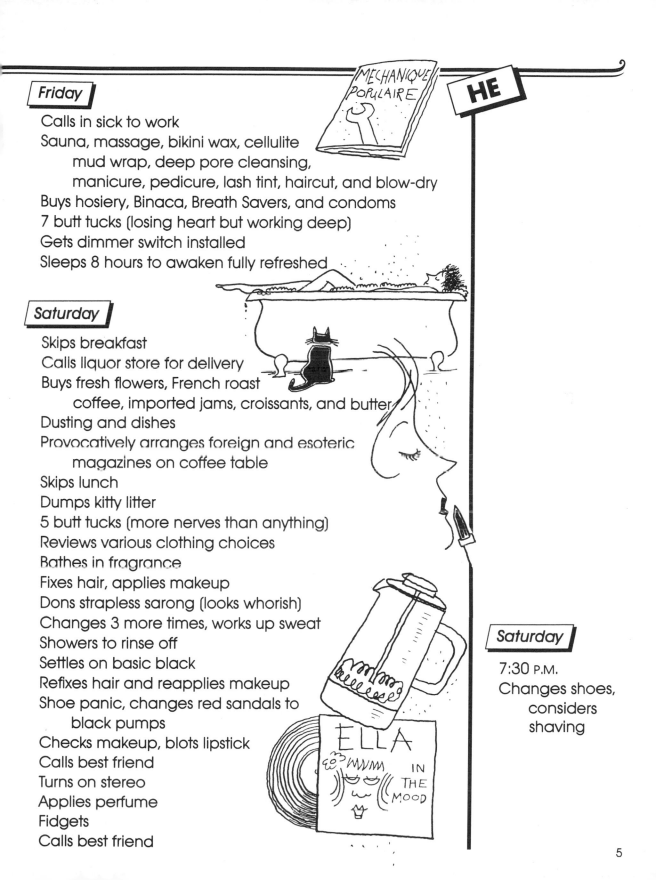

Saturday

Skips breakfast
Calls liquor store for delivery
Buys fresh flowers, French roast
    coffee, imported jams, croissants, and butter
Dusting and dishes
Provocatively arranges foreign and esoteric
    magazines on coffee table
Skips lunch
Dumps kitty litter
5 butt tucks (more nerves than anything)
Reviews various clothing choices
Bathes in fragrance
Fixes hair, applies makeup
Dons strapless sarong (looks whorish)
Changes 3 more times, works up sweat
Showers to rinse off
Settles on basic black
Refixes hair and reapplies makeup
Shoe panic, changes red sandals to
    black pumps
Checks makeup, blots lipstick
Calls best friend
Turns on stereo
Applies perfume
Fidgets
Calls best friend

Saturday

7:30 P.M.
Changes shoes,
    considers
    shaving

MECHANIQUE POPULAIRE

ELLA IN THE MOOD

5

PARTY PERCEPTIONS

SHE

In a room full of strangers,
SHE sees:

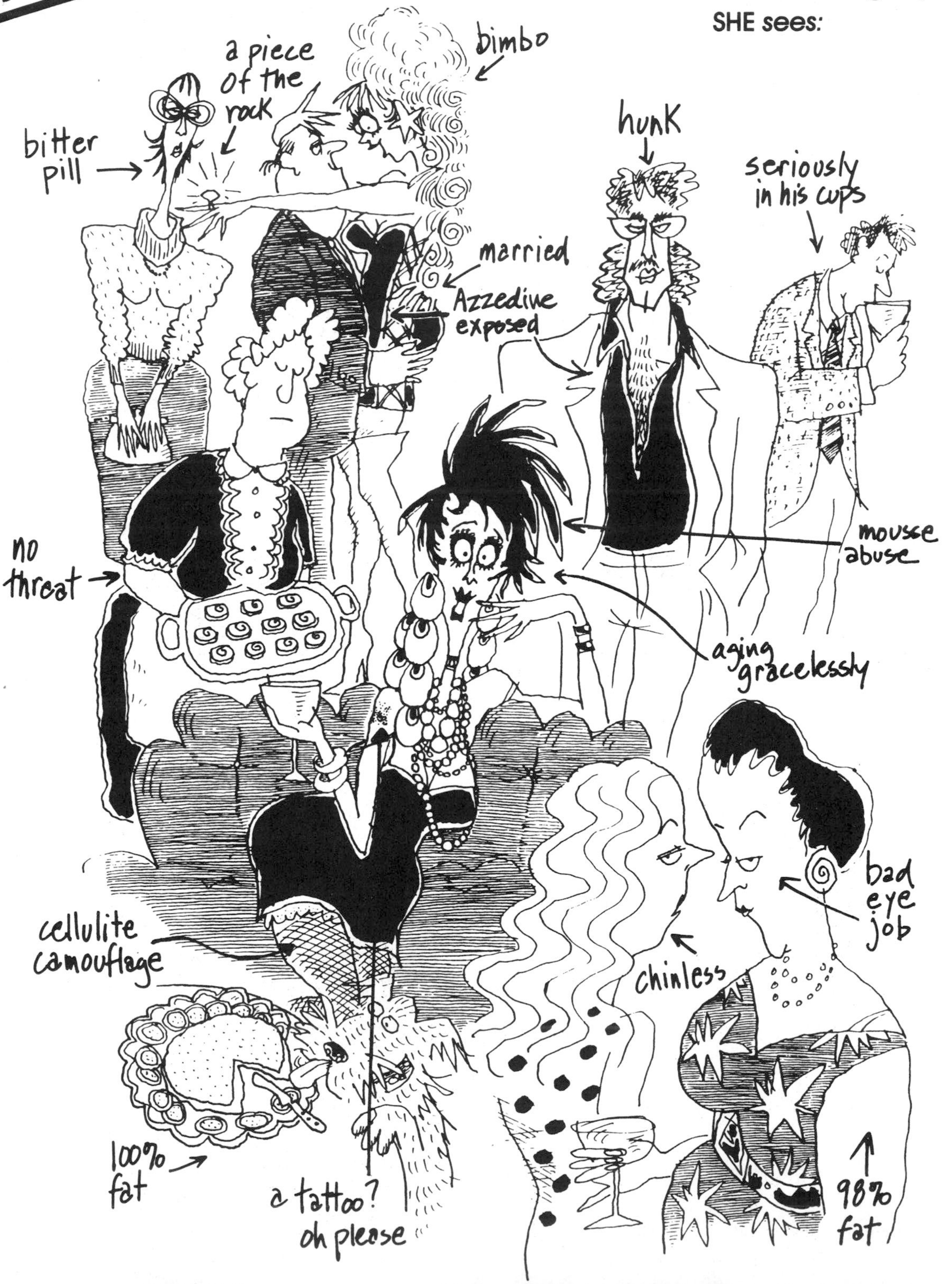

bimbo
a piece of the rock
bitter pill
hunk
seriously in his cups
married
Azzedine exposed
mousse abuse
no threat
aging gracelessly
bad eye job
cellulite camouflage
chinless
100% fat
a tattoo? oh please
98% fat

In a room full of strangers,
HE *sees:*

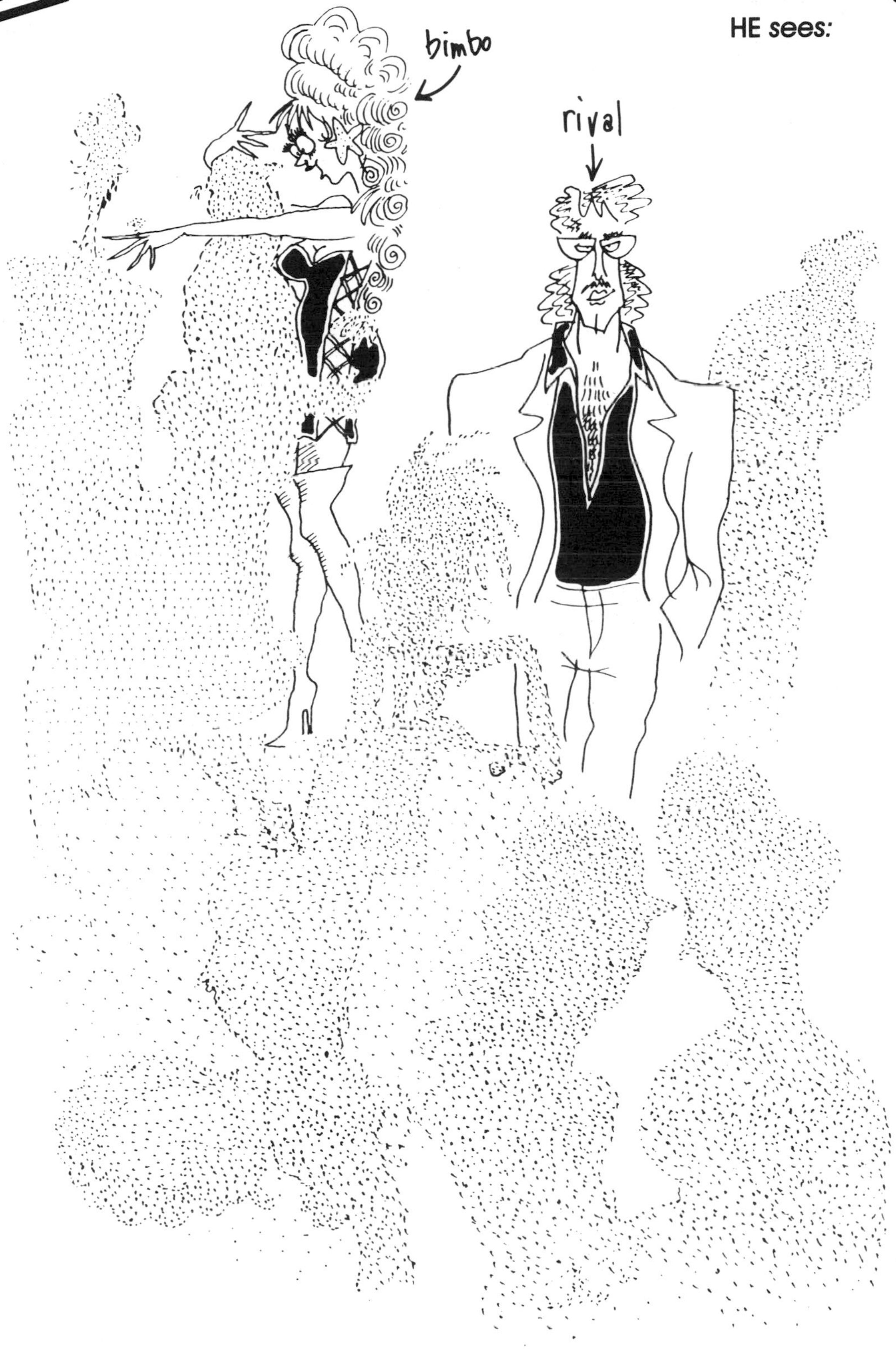
bimbo
rival

SHE

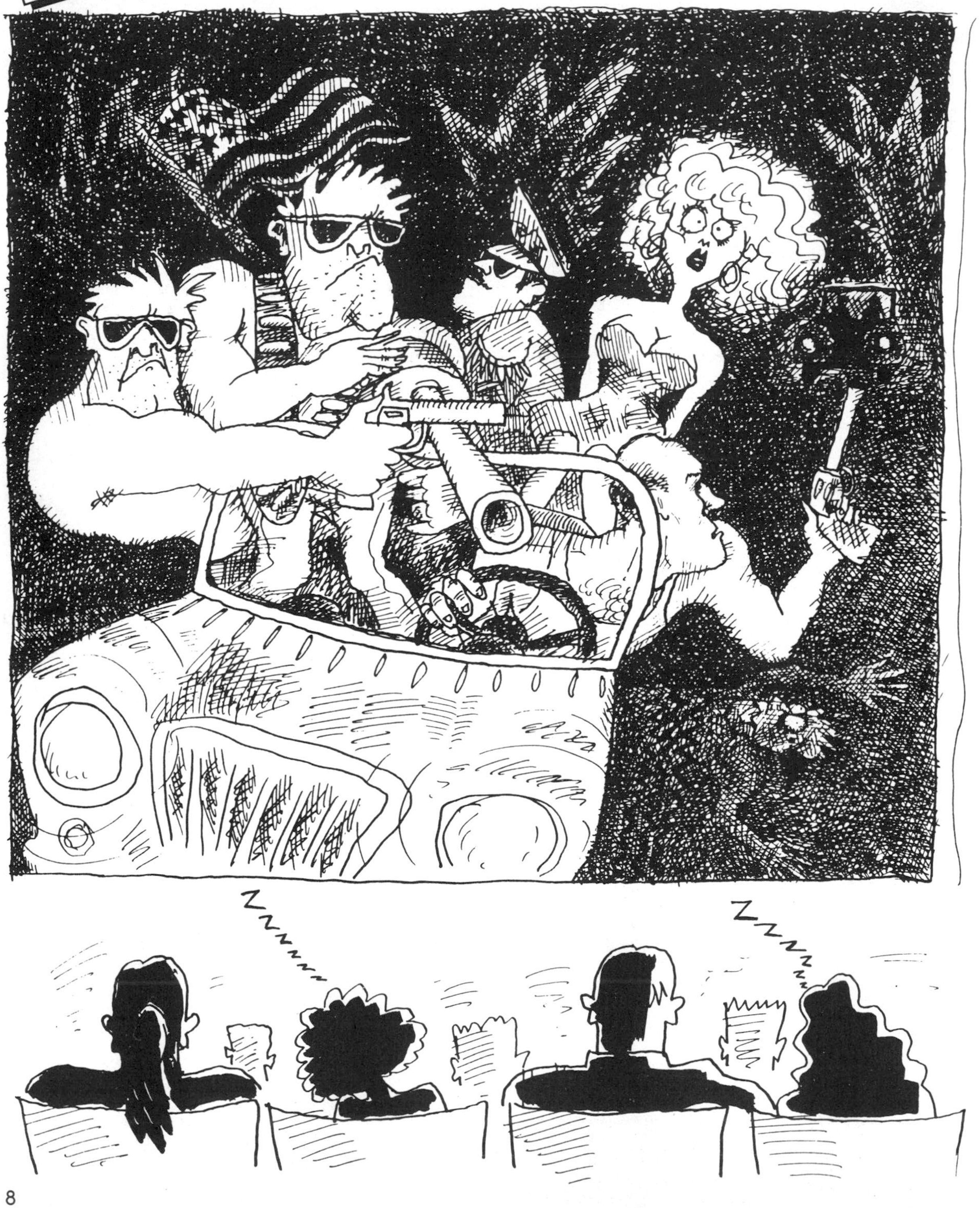

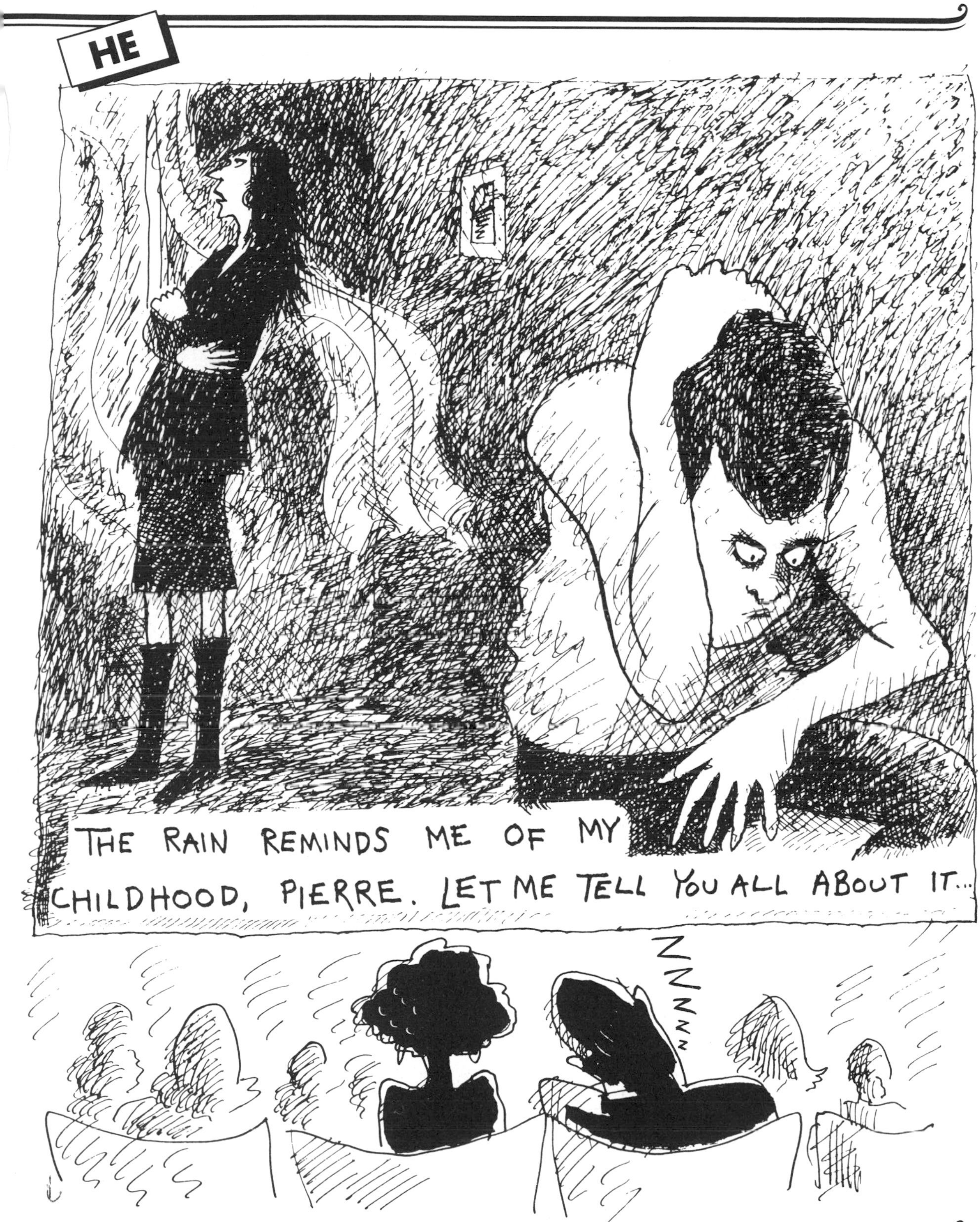
HE
THE RAIN REMINDS ME OF MY CHILDHOOD, PIERRE. LET ME TELL YOU ALL ABOUT IT...
ZZZZZ

DATE DENSITY

Where the available women are

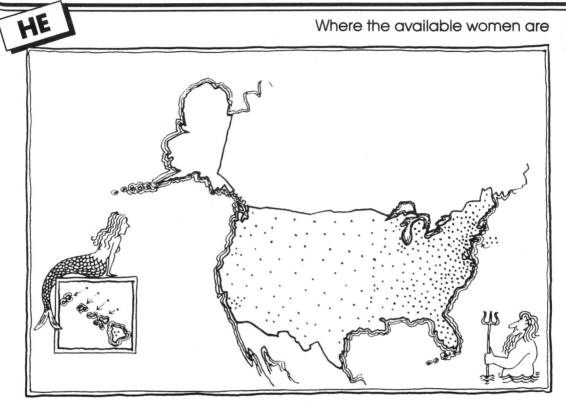

The ones you would want

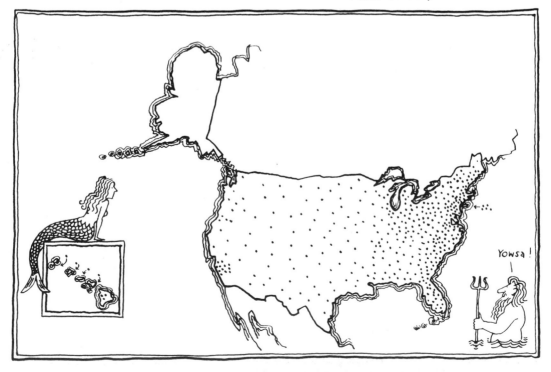

Where the available men are

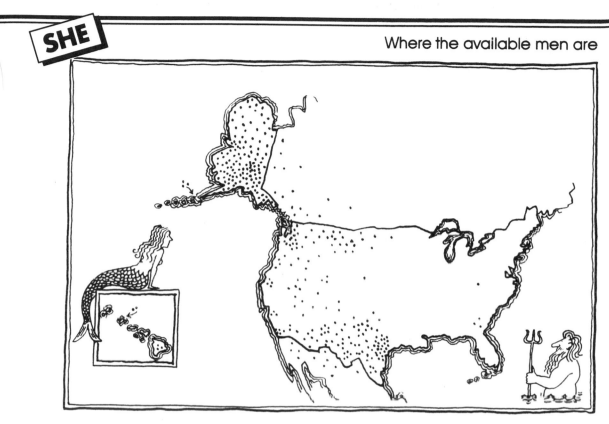

The ones you would want

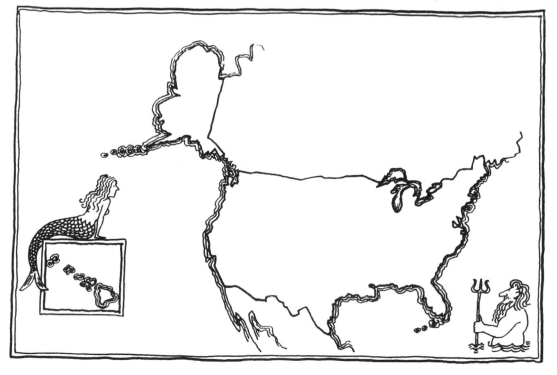

WHO PAYS?

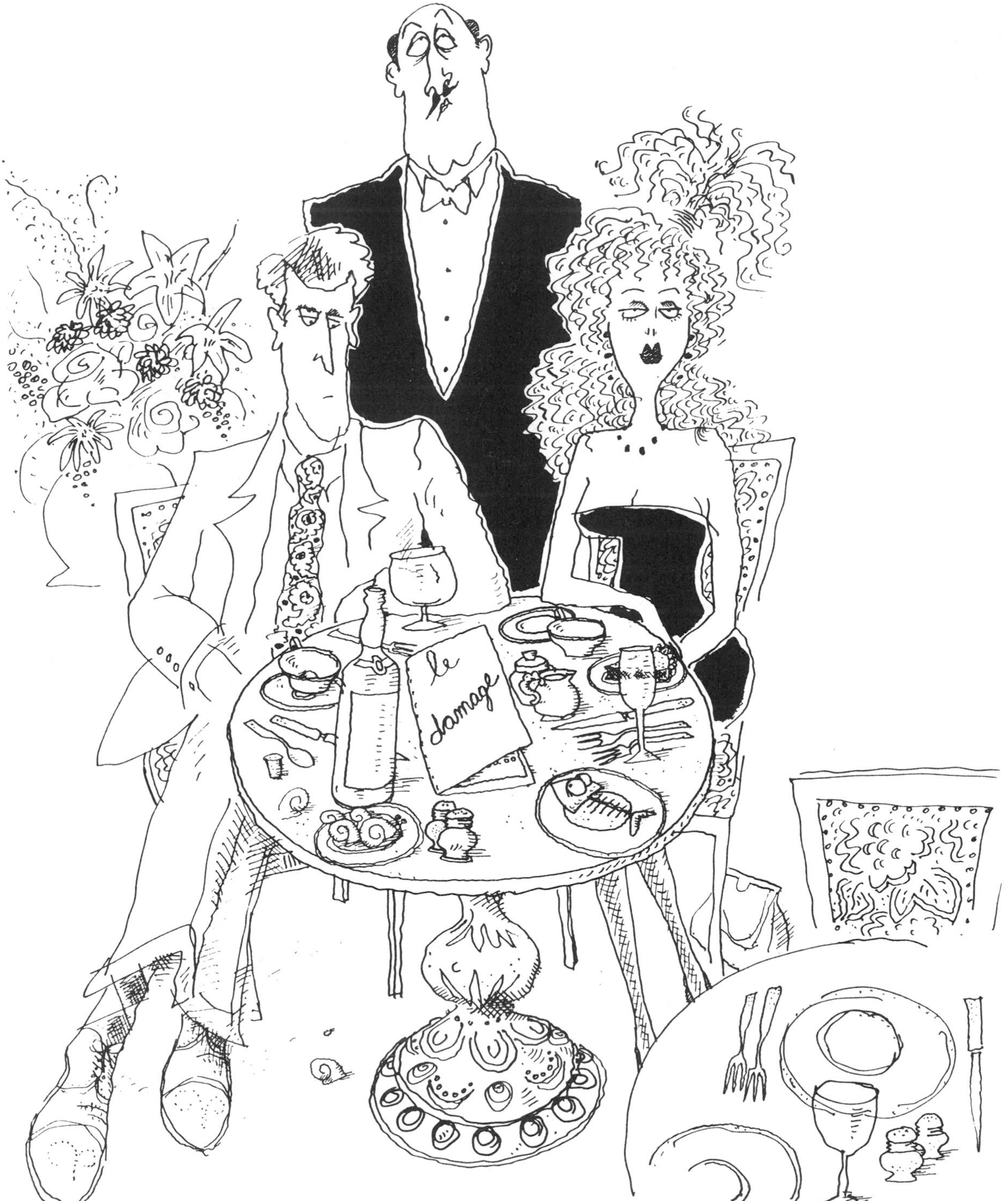
le damage

If *SHE* wants to sleep with him, then it's a date:
HE pays.

If *SHE* doesn't want to sleep with him and if *SHE's* a nice person who wants the "just friends" message to get through loud and clear:
SHE pays for herself and *insists* on it.

If *SHE* doesn't want to sleep with him and *SHE's* a nice person but *HE's* rich:
HE pays but *SHE* offers.

If *SHE* doesn't want to sleep with him, *SHE's* not a nice person, and *HE's* rich:
HE pays.

If *SHE* doesn't want to sleep with him, *SHE's* not a nice person, and *HE's* not rich:
HE pays.

If *HE* pays but *SHE* doesn't want to seem like a freeloader:
SHE offers to help, *HE* refuses, *SHE* says she'll get the drinks or coffee later.

If *HE's* cheap:
HE asks her to split the bill.

If *HE's* broke, they're close, *SHE's* not a nice person, and they're going to a good place:
SHE feigns indifference to the financial catastrophe that awaits him. *HE* pays.

If *HE's* broke, they're close, *SHE's* a nice person, and they're going to a good place:
SHE slips him the money before they get to the restaurant.

If *HE's* broke, they're close, *SHE's* nice, and they're going to a cheap place:
SHE pays.

If *HE's* broke, they're close, *SHE's* not nice, and they're going to a cheap place:
SHE suddenly realizes that *SHE* has to stay home to wash her hair . . . forever.

If *SHE* asked him out, it's his birthday, and they're in love:
SHE pays.

If *SHE* asked him out and it's not his birthday but *HE* knows what's good for him:
SHE starts to pay, *HE* protests, *SHE* gives in.

If *HE's* a guy with any interest in seeing her again:
HE pays. Period.

continued

If *SHE's* alone:
SHE pays.

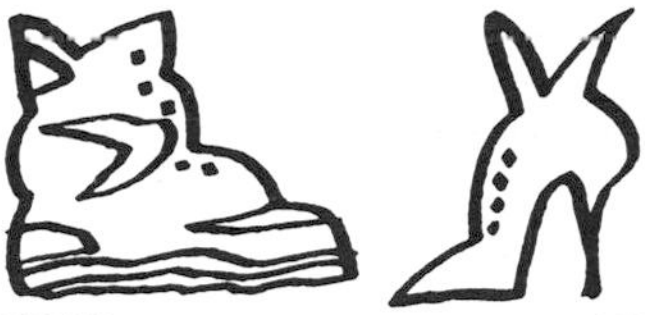

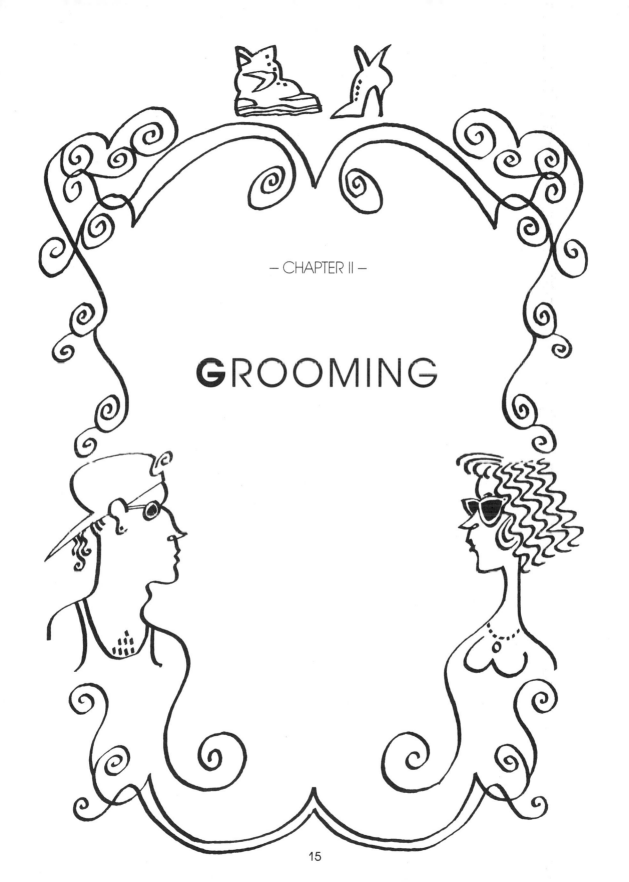

— CHAPTER II —

GROOMING

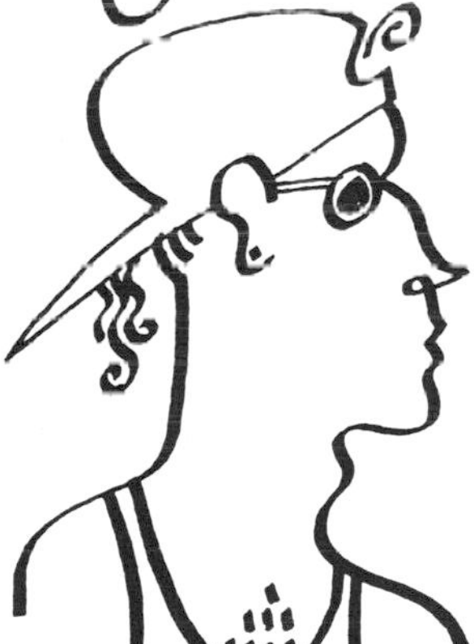

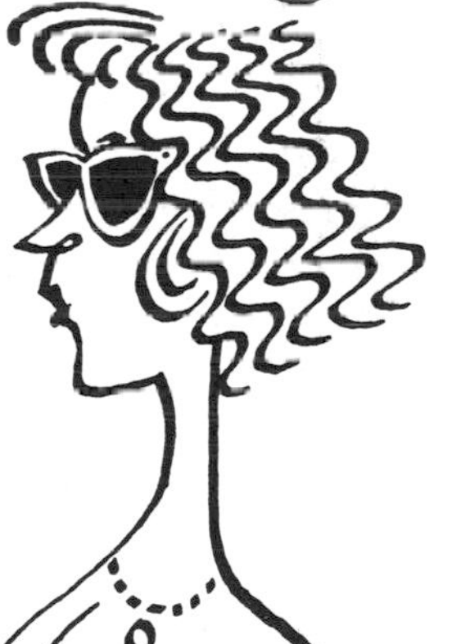

MIRROR IMAGE

SHE

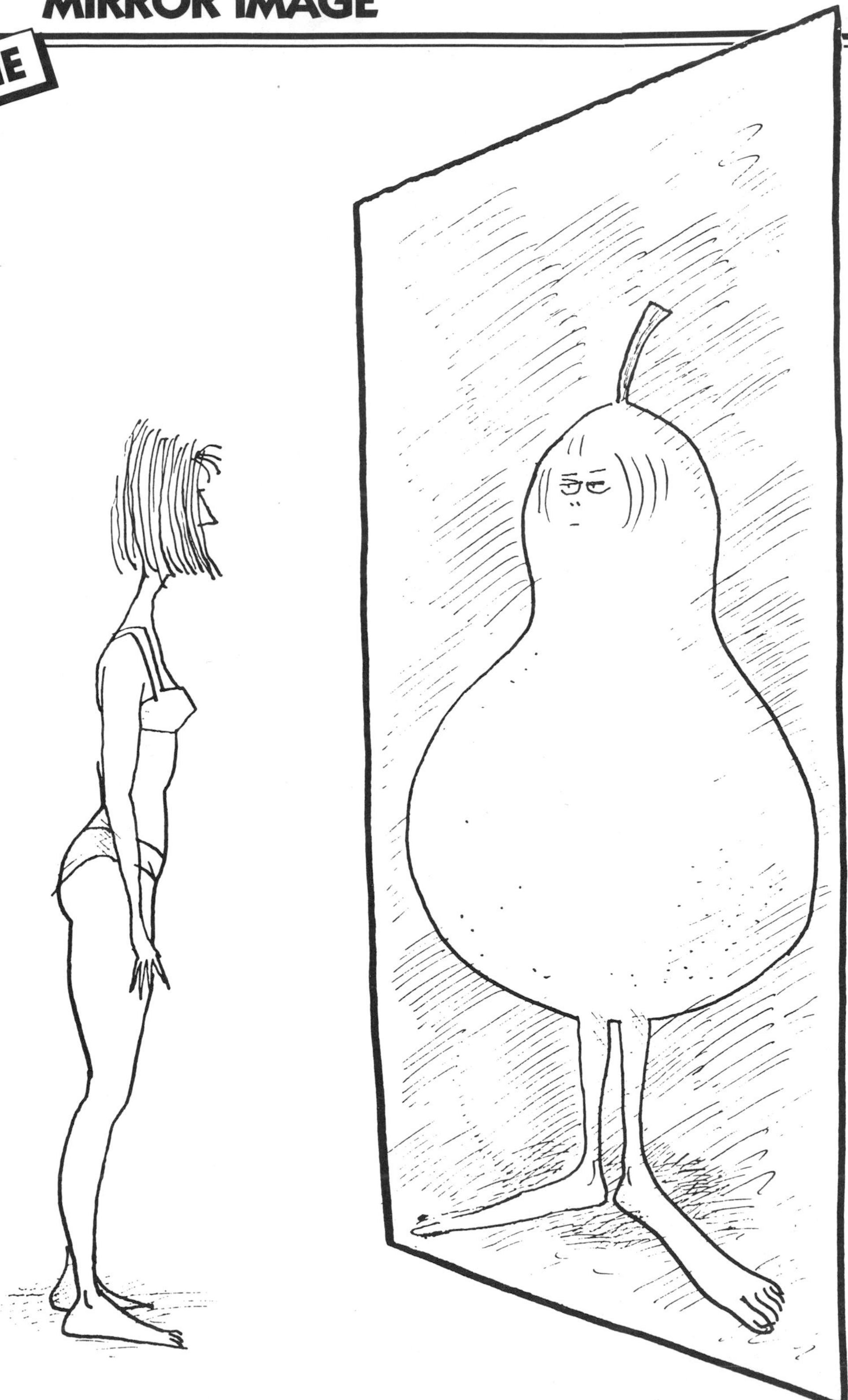

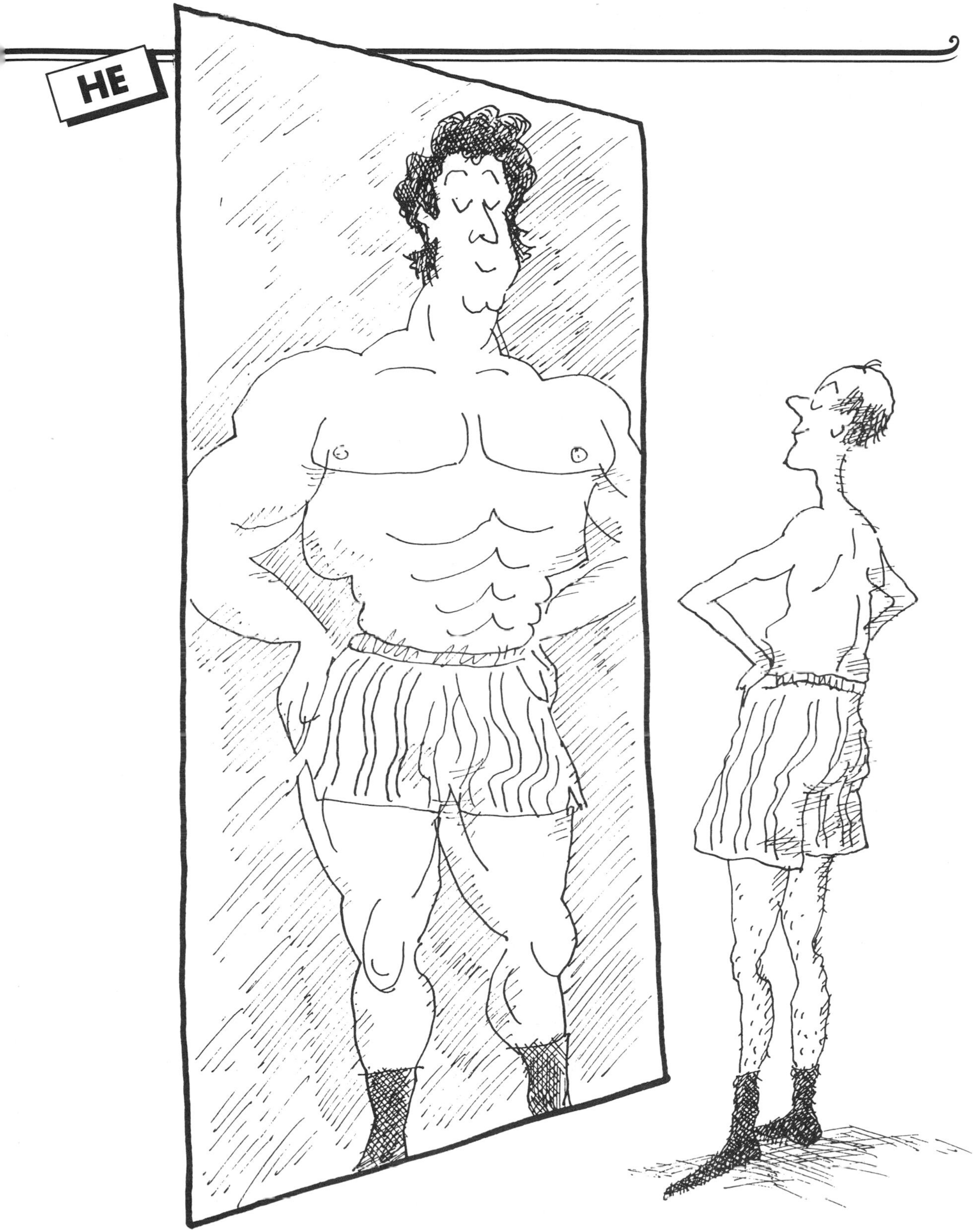
HE

HAIRY WISH LIST

HE

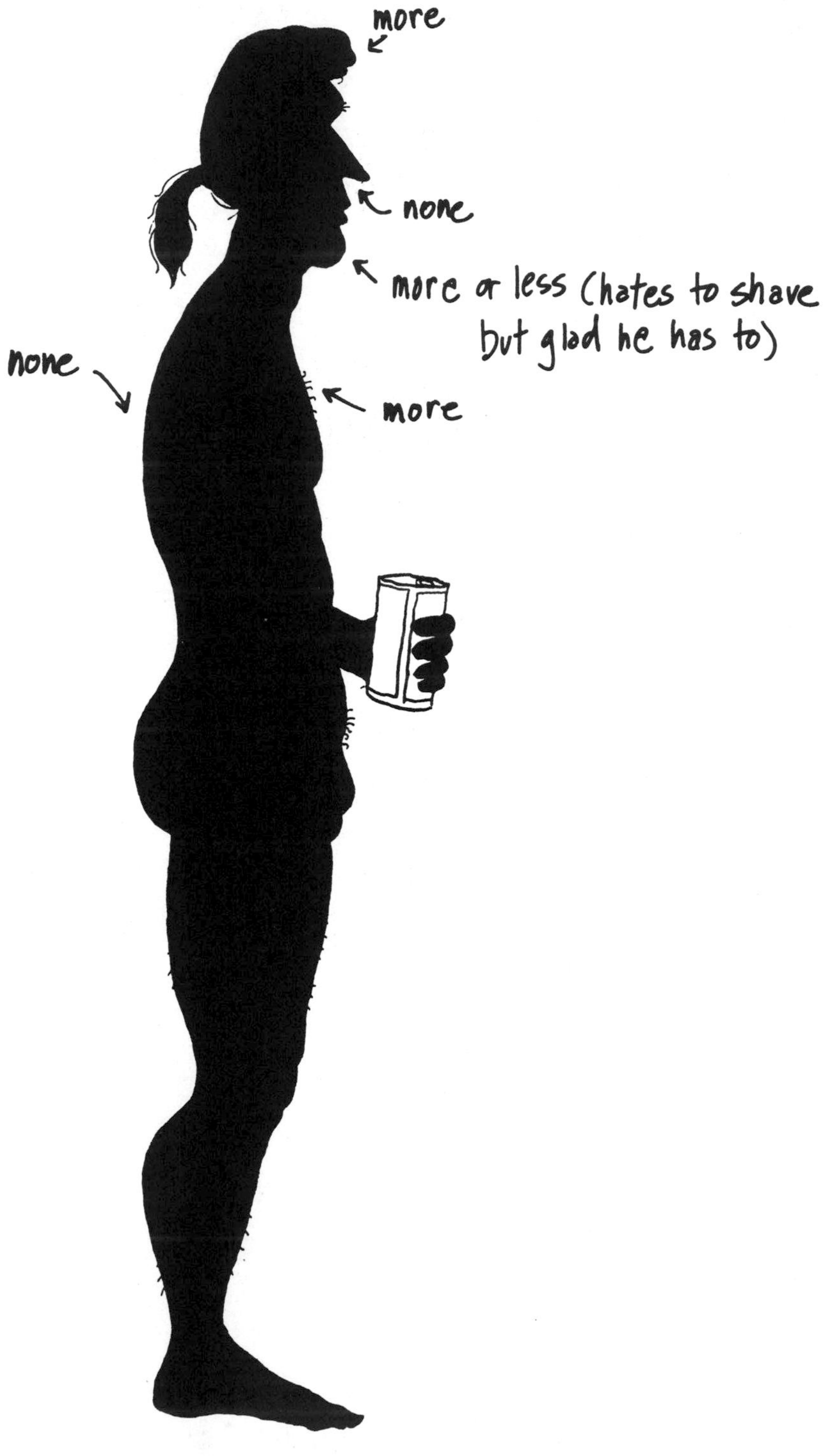
more
none
more or less (hates to shave but glad he has to)
none
more

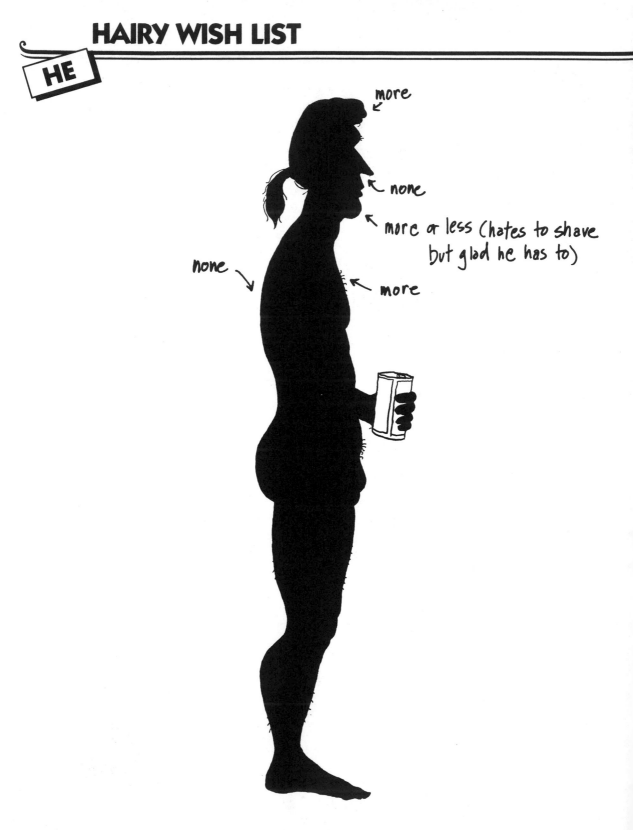

SHE

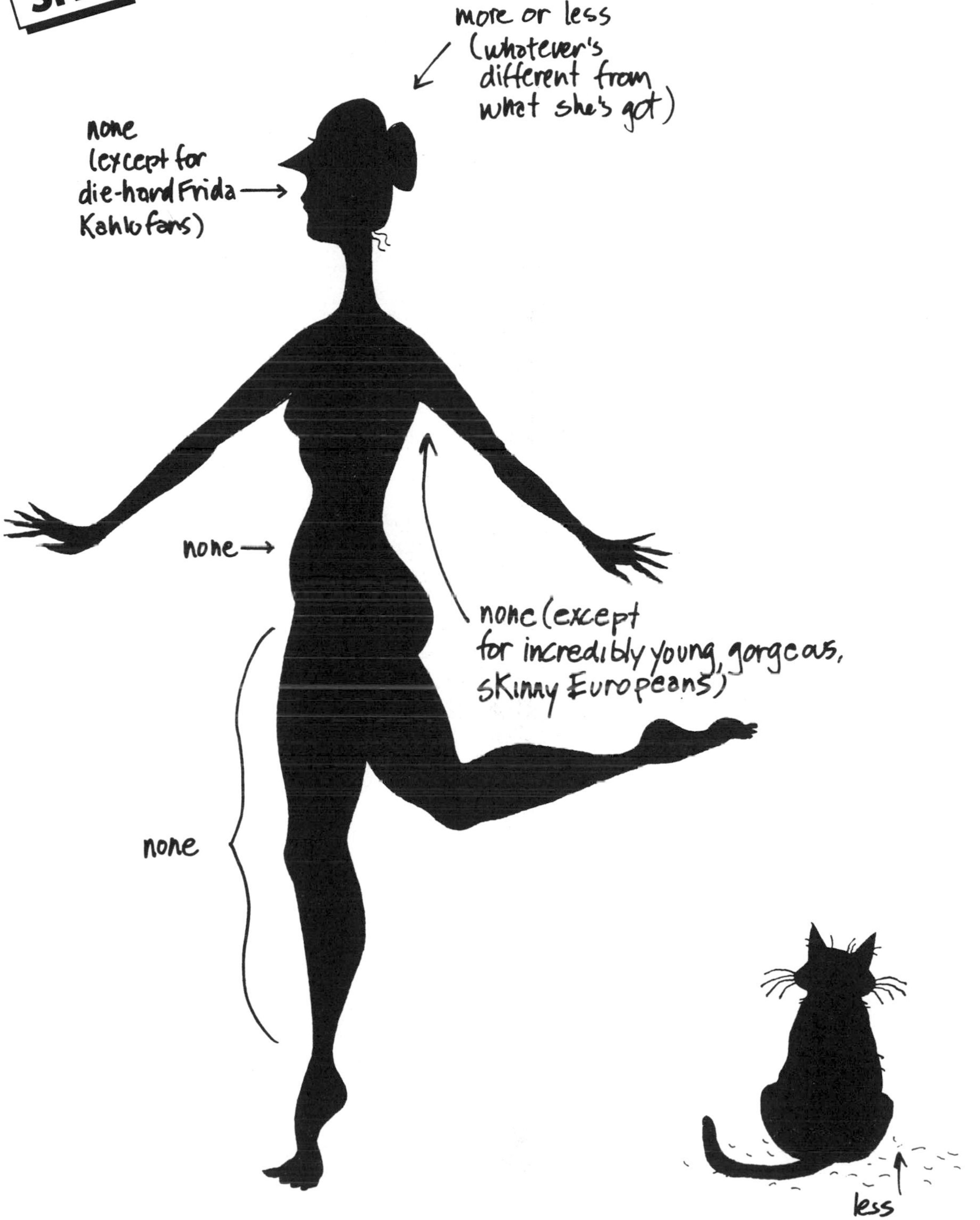

more or less (whatever's different from what she's got)
none (except for die-hard Frida Kahlo fans)
none
none (except for incredibly young, gorgeous, skinny Europeans)
none
less

SHOPPING DYNAMICS

HE

EXIT

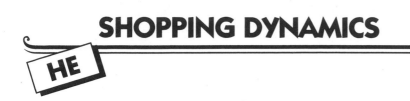

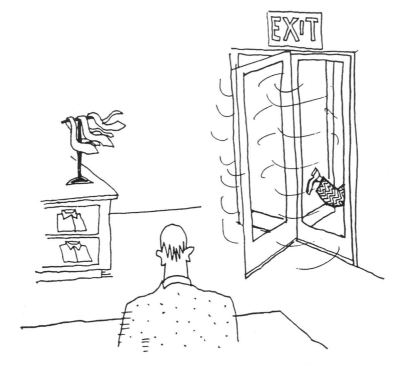

1) Finding it fast

2) Getting the hell out of the store

SHE

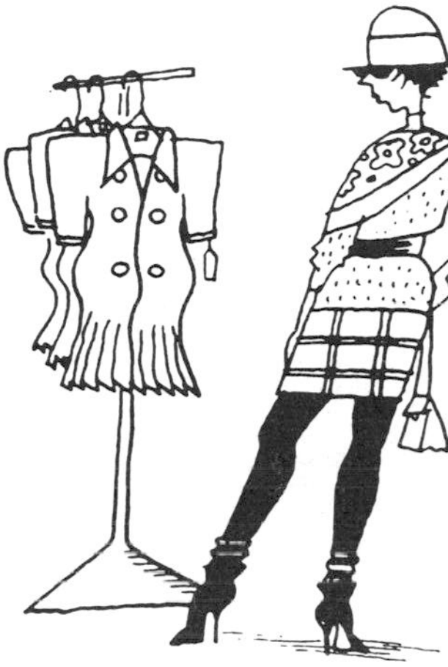

1) Finding it

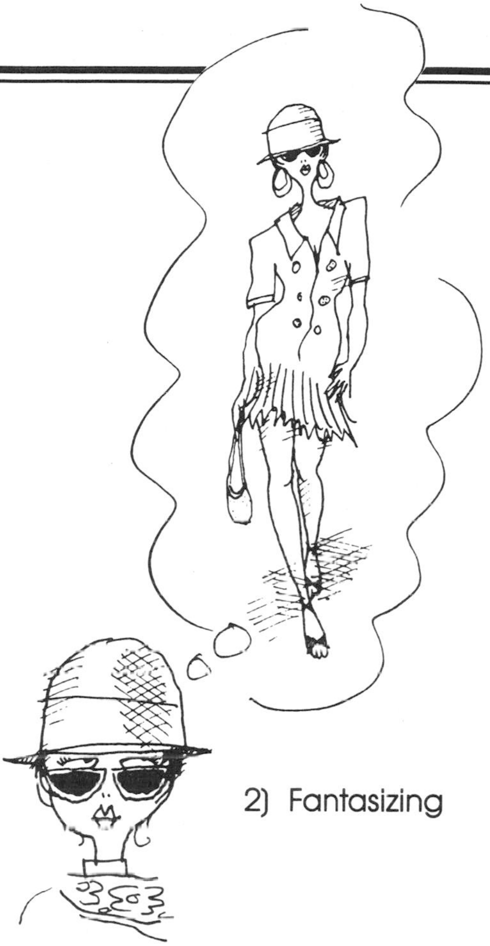

2) Fantasizing

3) Finding it cheaper in another store

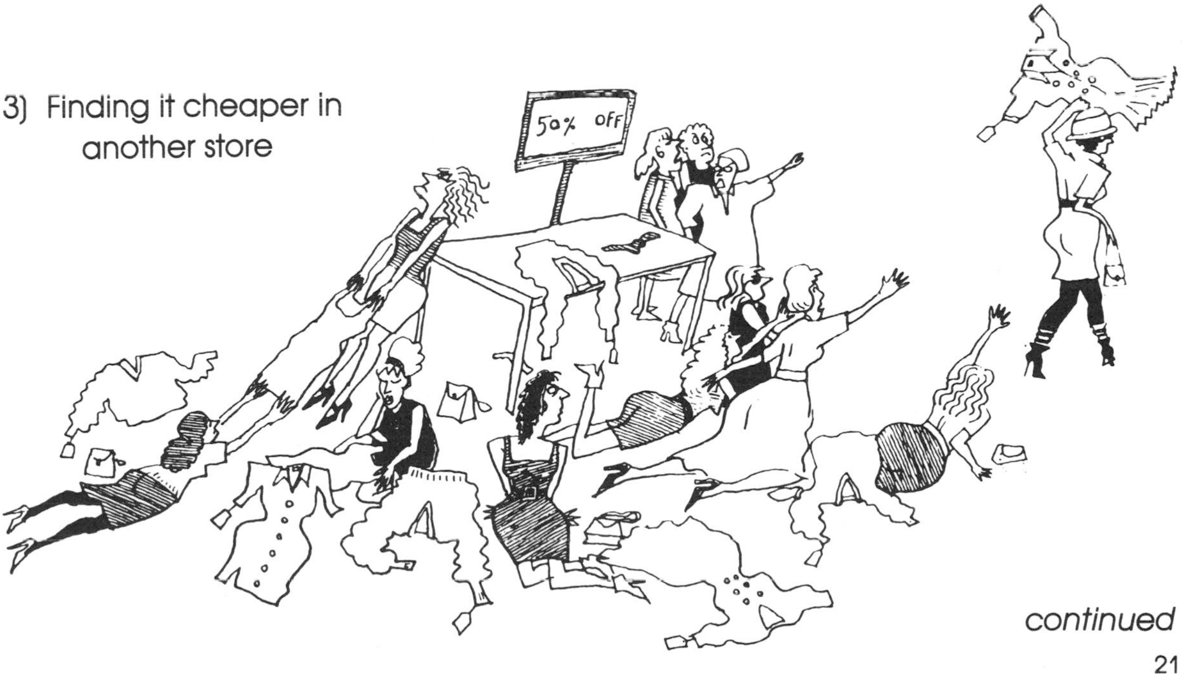
50% OFF

continued

SHOPPING DYNAMICS *Continued*

SHE

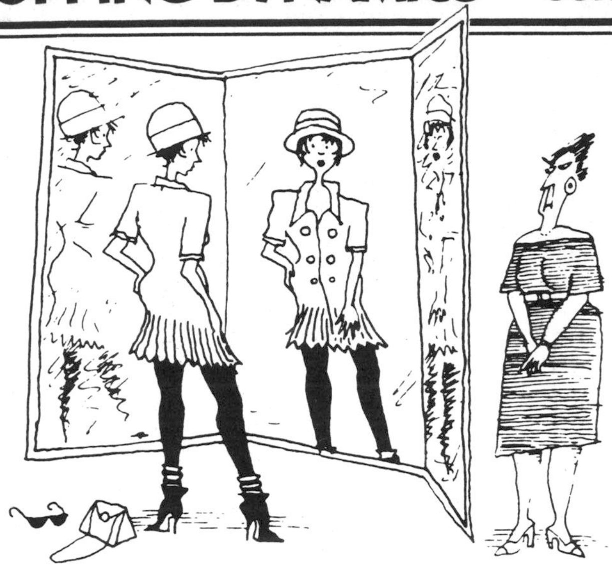

4) Trying it on

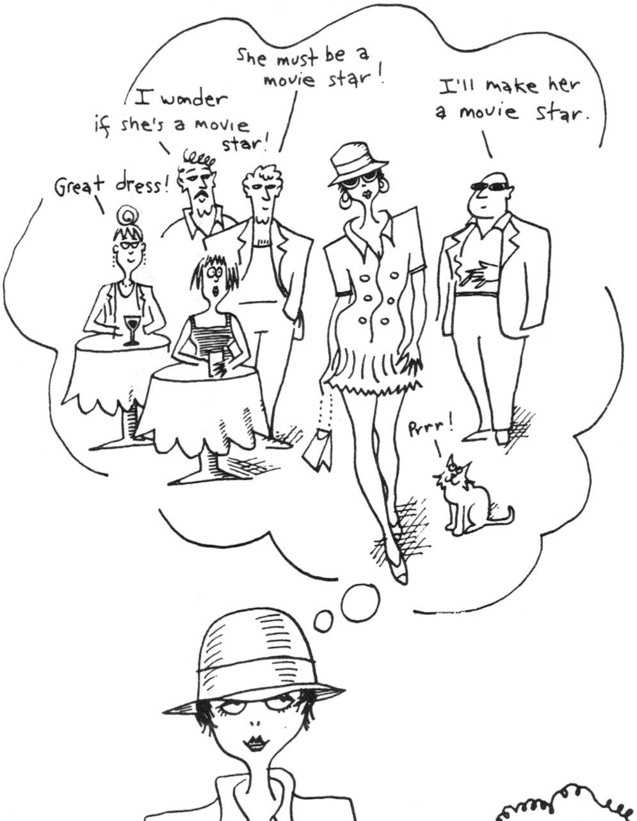
She must be a movie star!
I wonder if she's a movie star!
I'll make her a movie star.
Great dress!
Prrr!

5) More fantasizing

6) Spreading the word

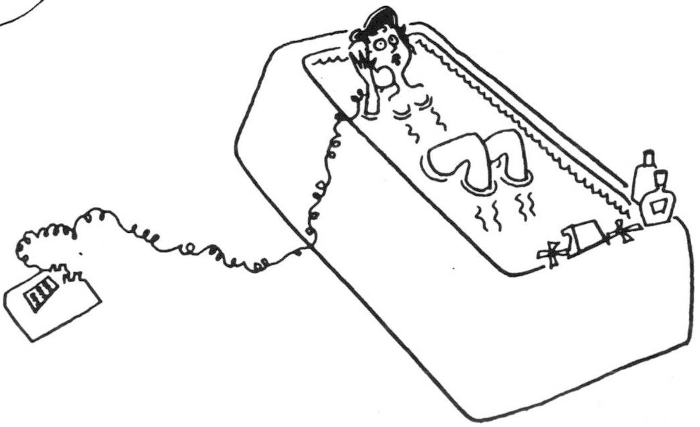

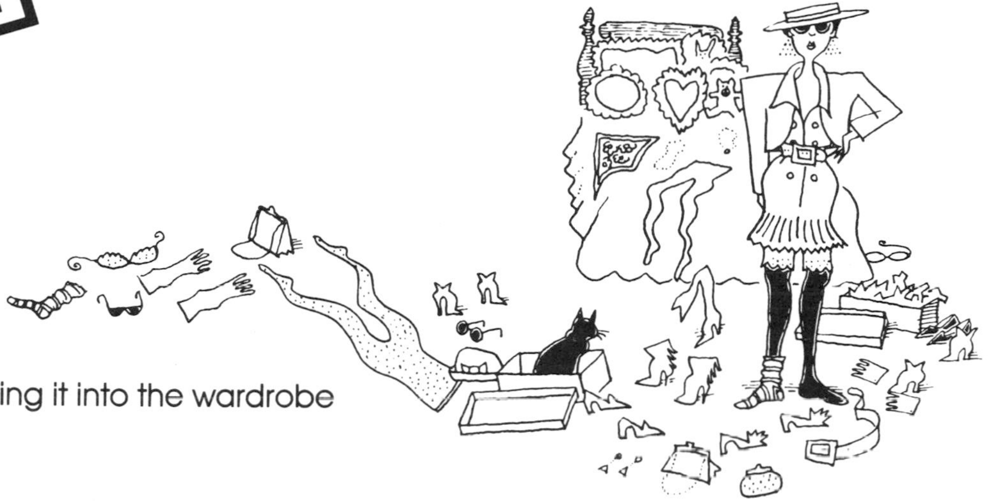

7) Working it into the wardrobe

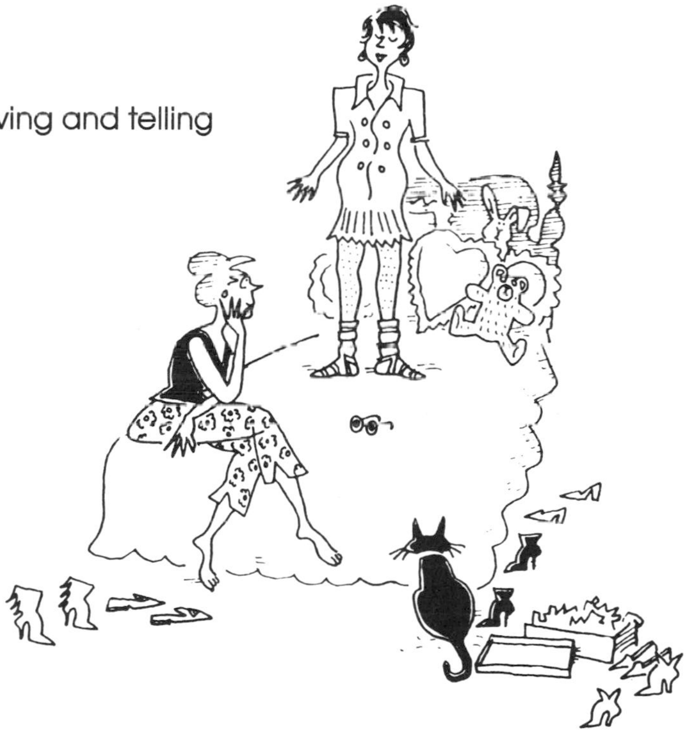

8) Showing and telling

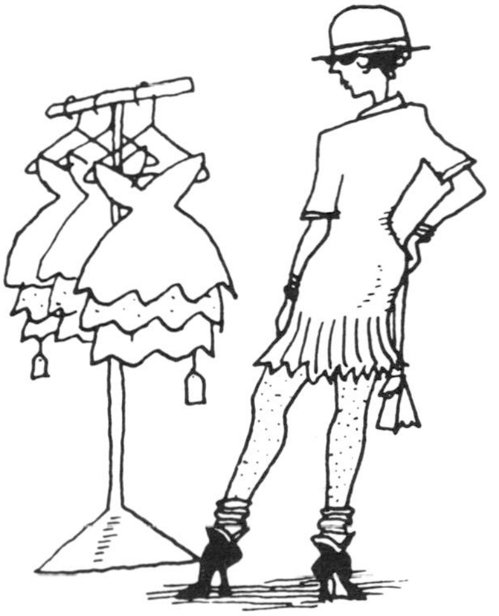

9) Wearing

HE

FOOTNOTES

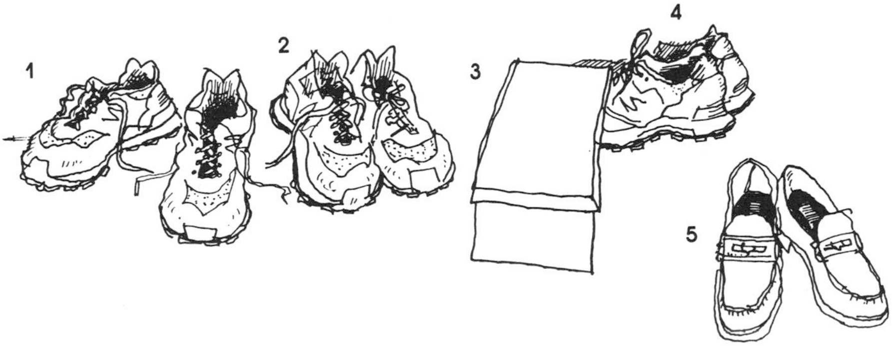
1
2
3
4
5

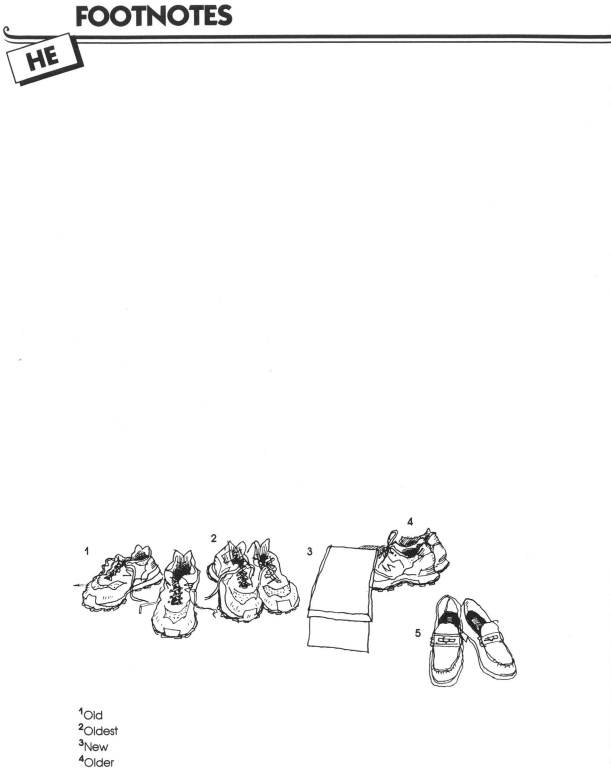

[1]Old
[2]Oldest
[3]New
[4]Older
[5]Work

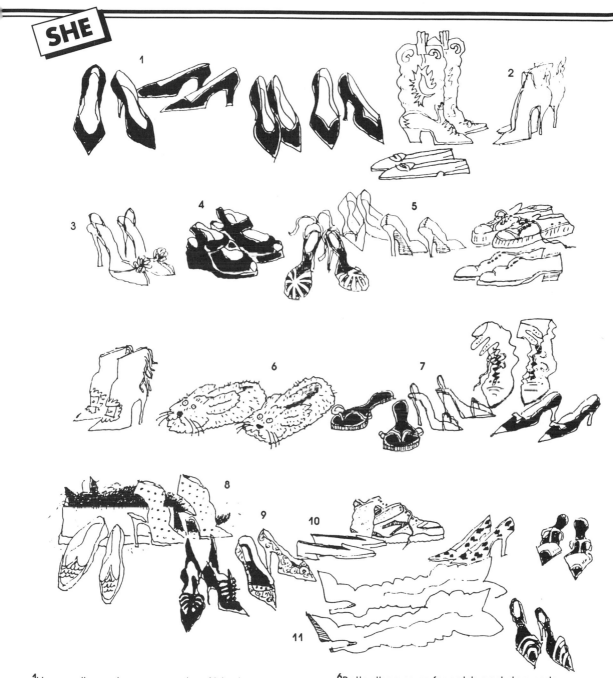

¹You can't own too many pairs of black pumps

²Good for the ego because you don't have to lose weight to try them on

³On sale for $20, marked down from $95, so by buying these an *actual profit* of $75 has been realized

⁴Minnie Mouse platforms, clunky but make the thighs look thinner

⁵Too small, need stretching

⁶Better than soup for colds and depression

⁷Make you look like you're getting a lot of what you're not getting any of

⁸These go with nothing but they're art that walks

⁹*Peau de soies,* dyed to match for cousin's wedding and never worn again

¹⁰Lizard flats for short dates (endangered species?)

¹¹These boots were not made for walking

BASIC BLACK *Why Do You Wear It?*

SHE

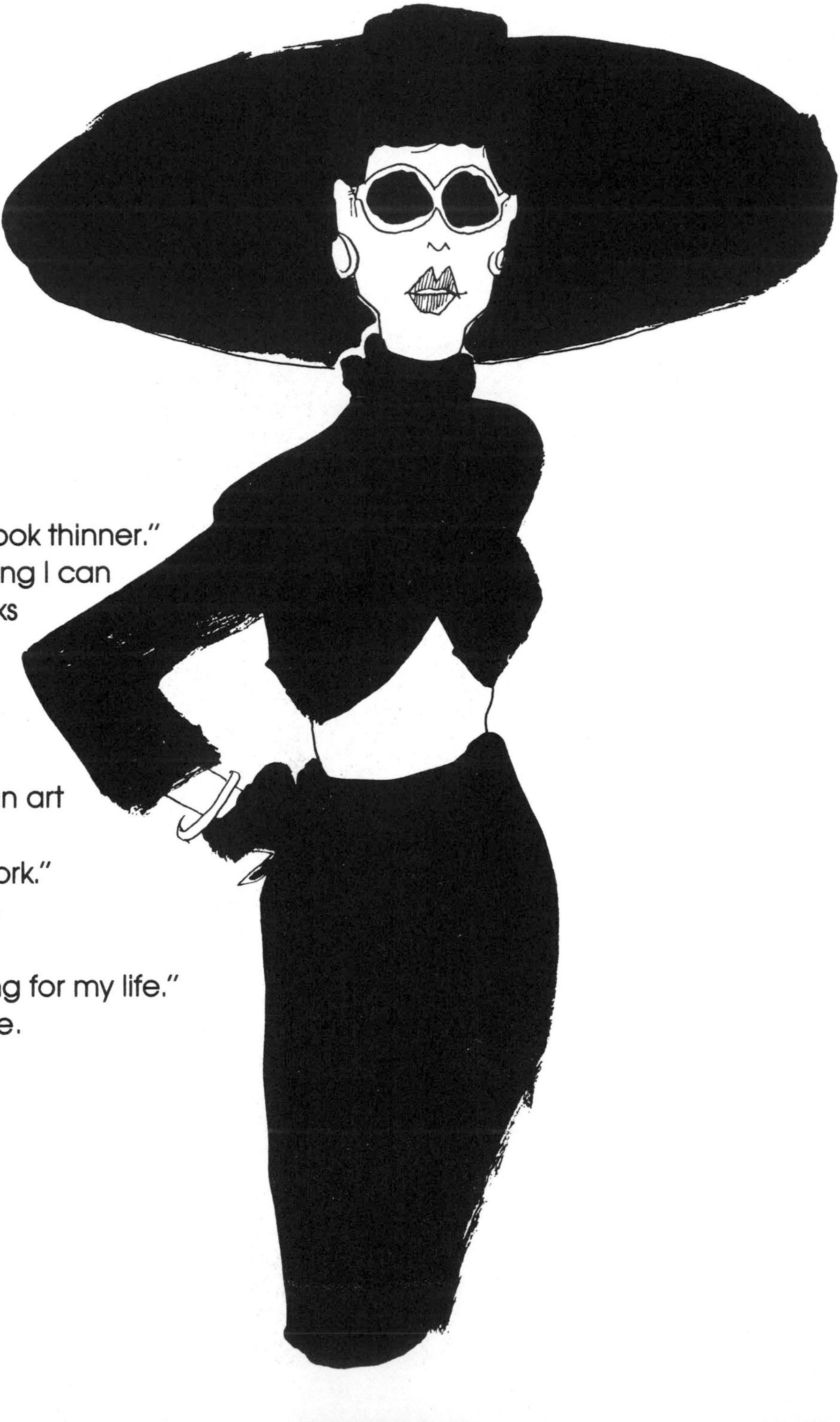

1) "It makes me look thinner."
2) "It's the only thing I can afford that looks expensive."
3) "It's sexy."
4) "It's easy to accessorize."
5) "I'm going to an art opening."
6) "I live in New York."
7) "I wish I lived in New York."
8) "I'm in mourning for my life."
9) All of the above.

1) "I thought it was navy blue."

UNDER EVERYTHING

HE

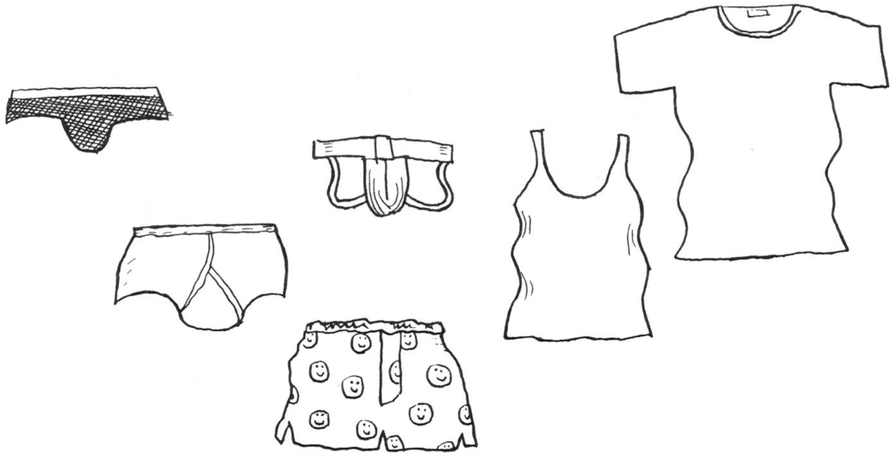

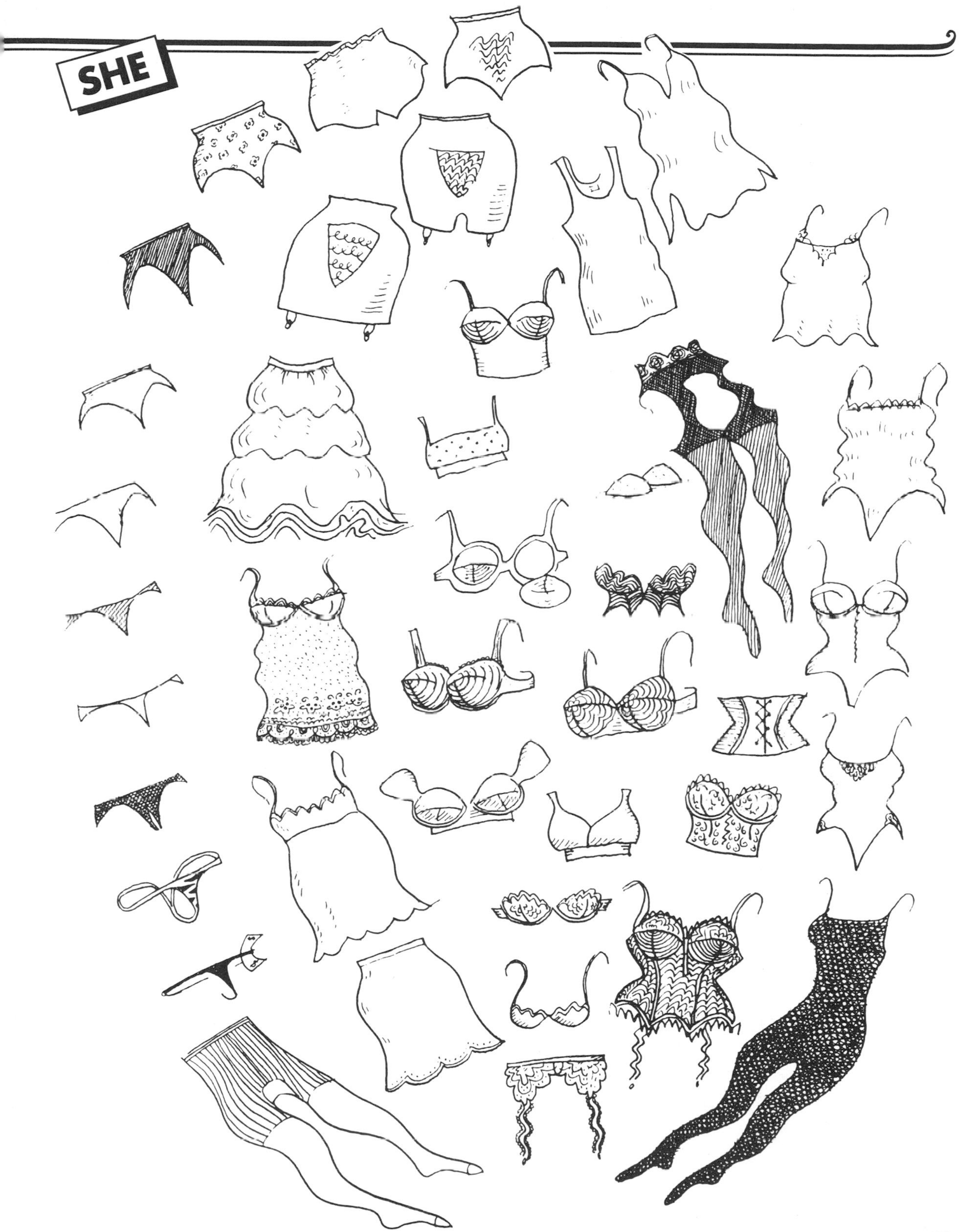
SHE

FASHION STATEMENTS

HE

What it means when HE *wears her clothes:*

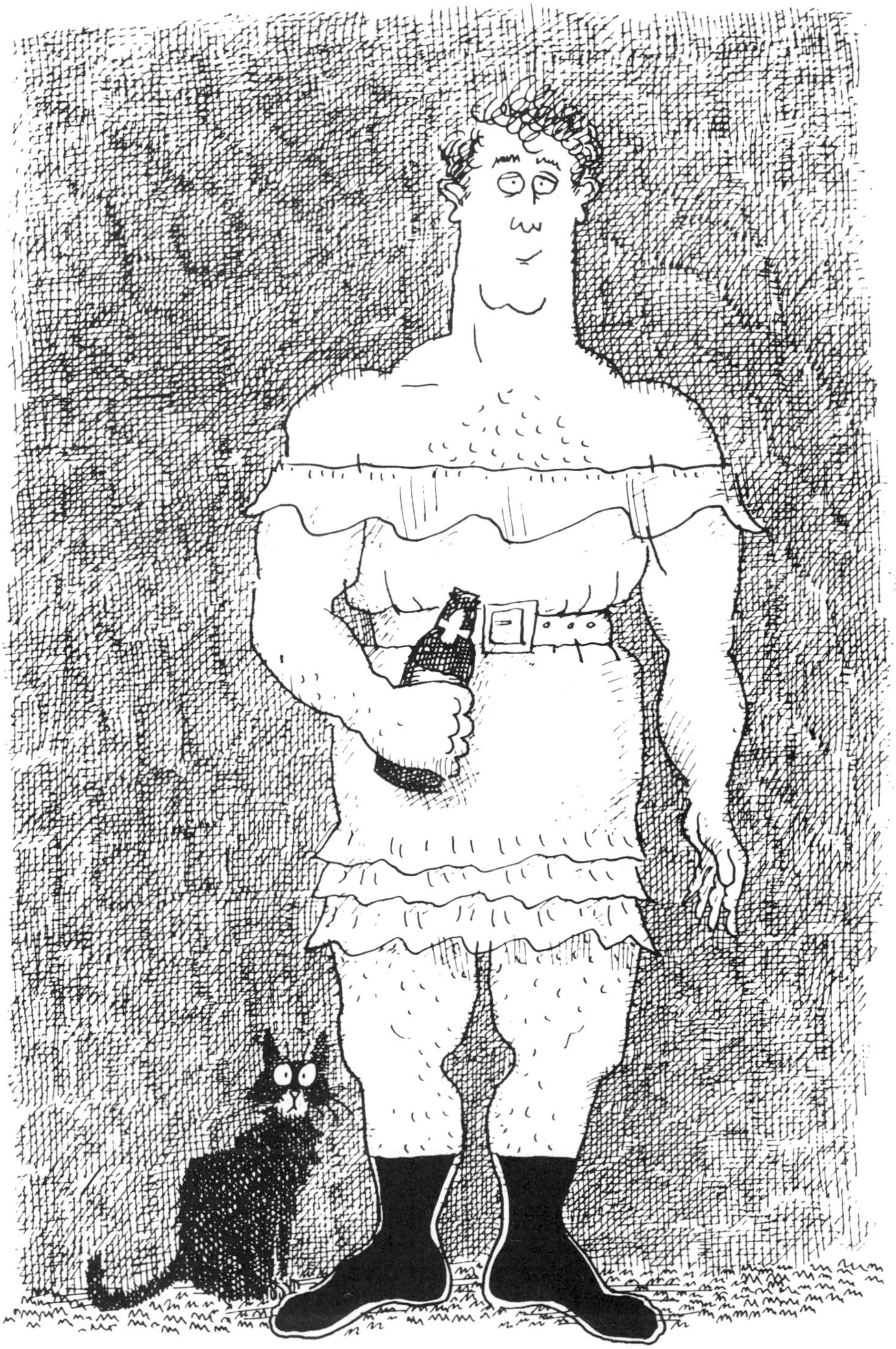

HE's *a sicko.*

SHE

What it means when SHE *wears his clothes:*

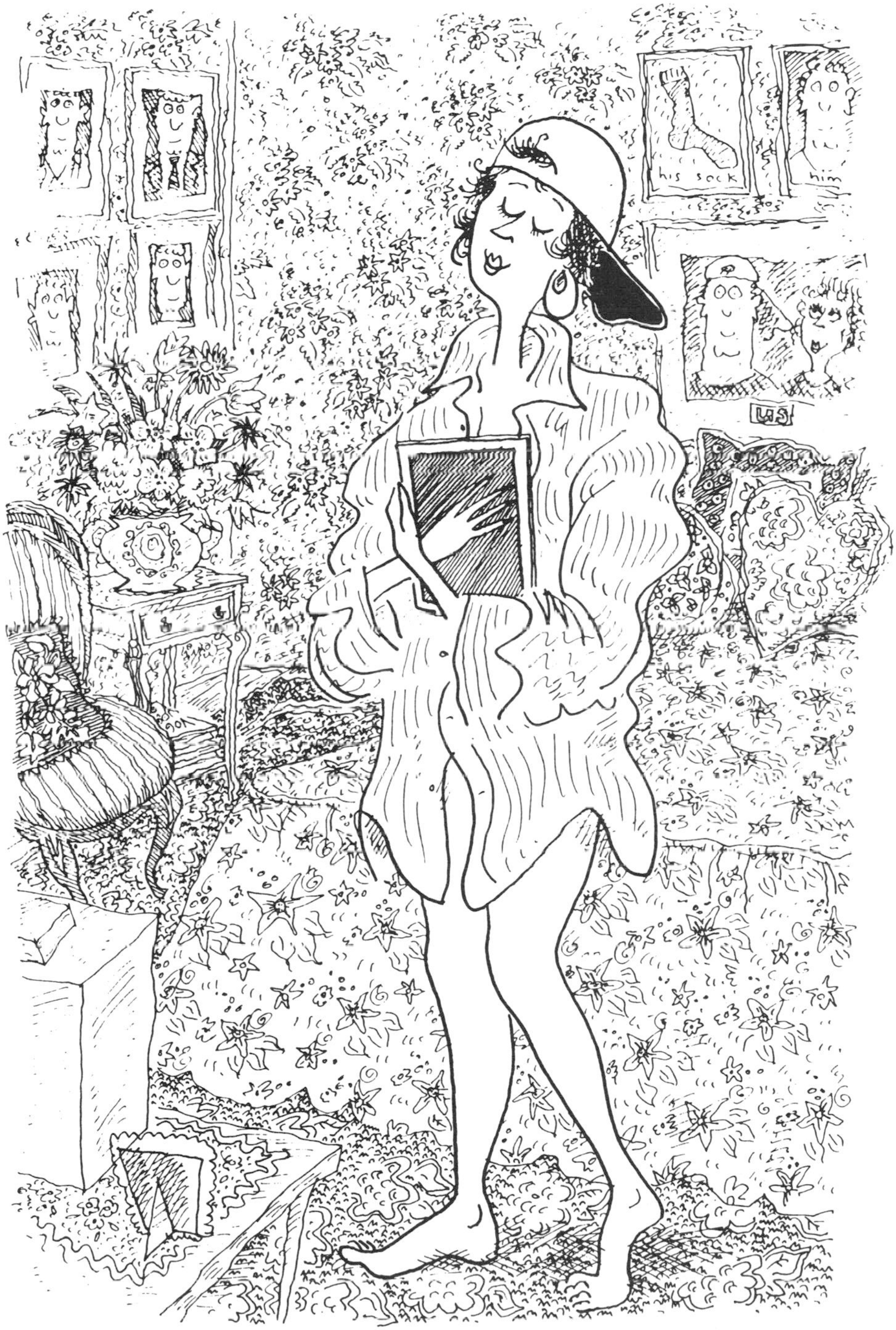
his sock
him

SHE*'s in love.*

PORTABLE NECESSITIES OF LIFE

HE

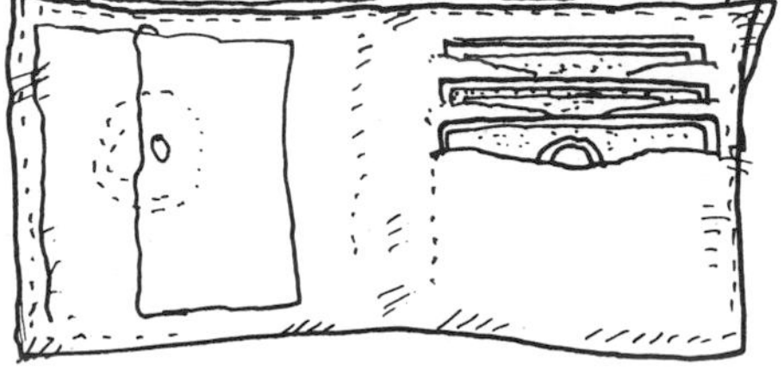

Has a wallet (cash and carry)

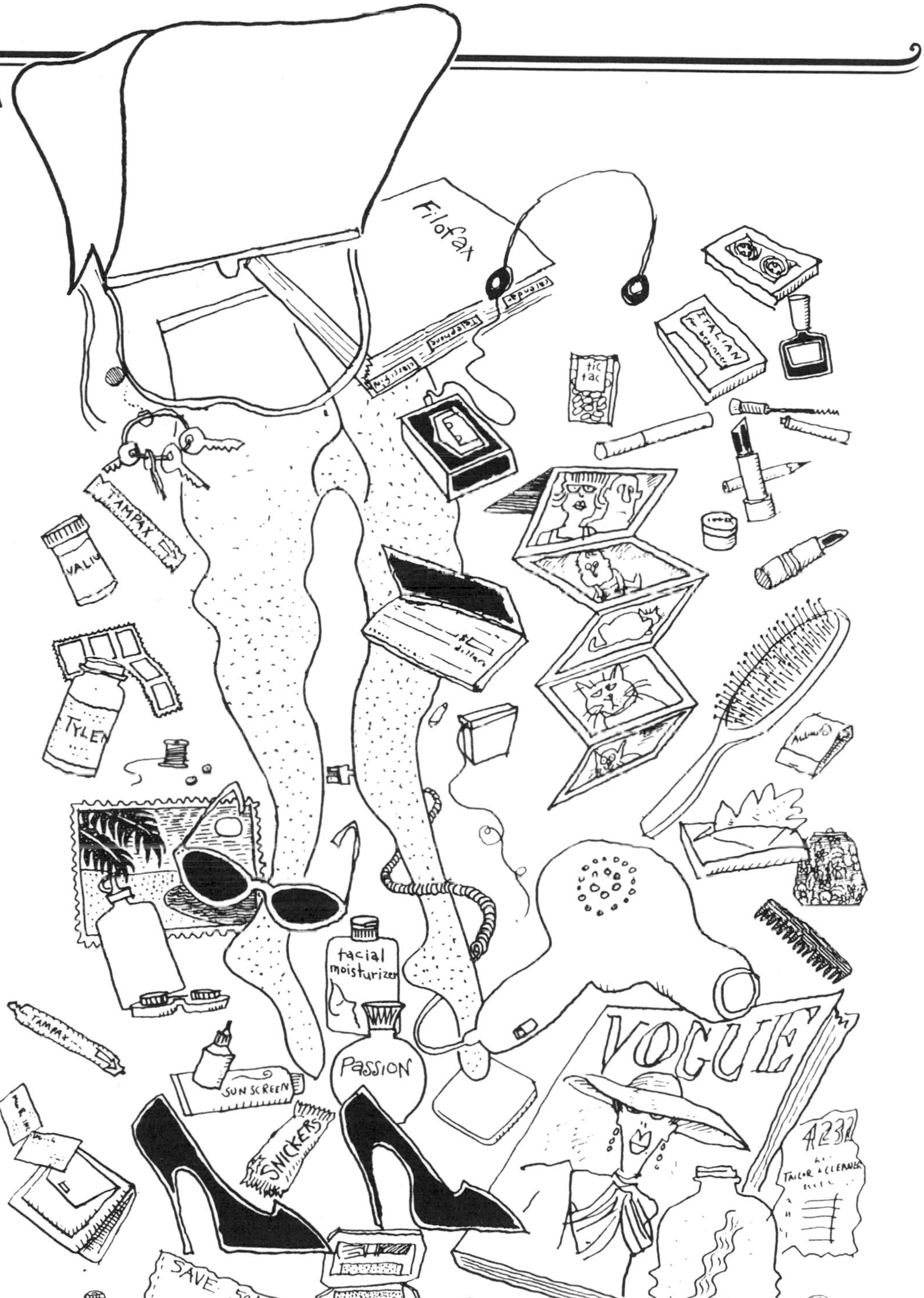
Filofax
TAMPAX
VALIU
tic tac
ITALIAN
TYLE
facial moisturizer
PASSION
SUN SCREEN
SNICKERS
VOGUE
SAVE 50¢
evian

Carries a purse (you never know when there's going to be a monsoon)

THE MEANING OF FAT

HE

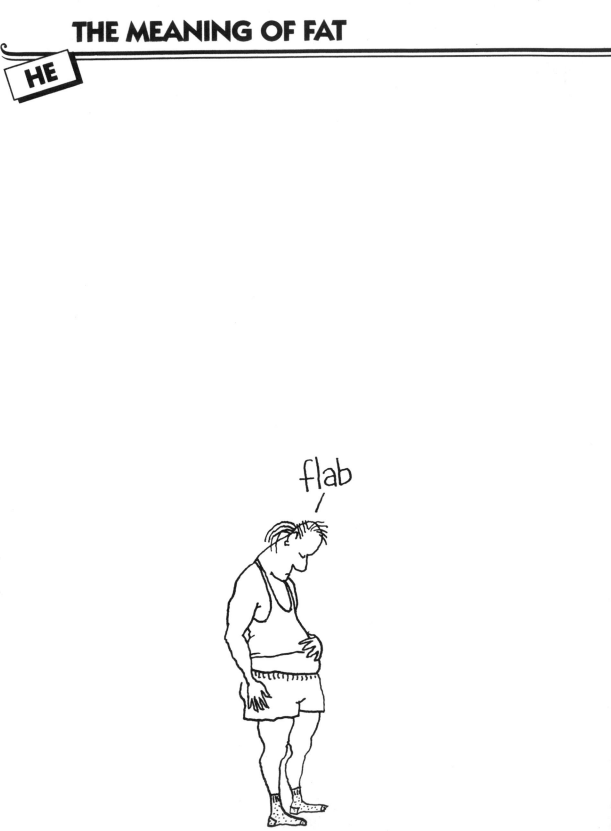

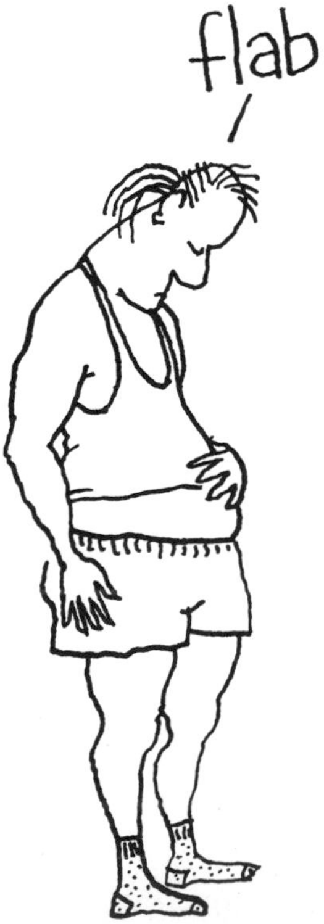
flab

SHE

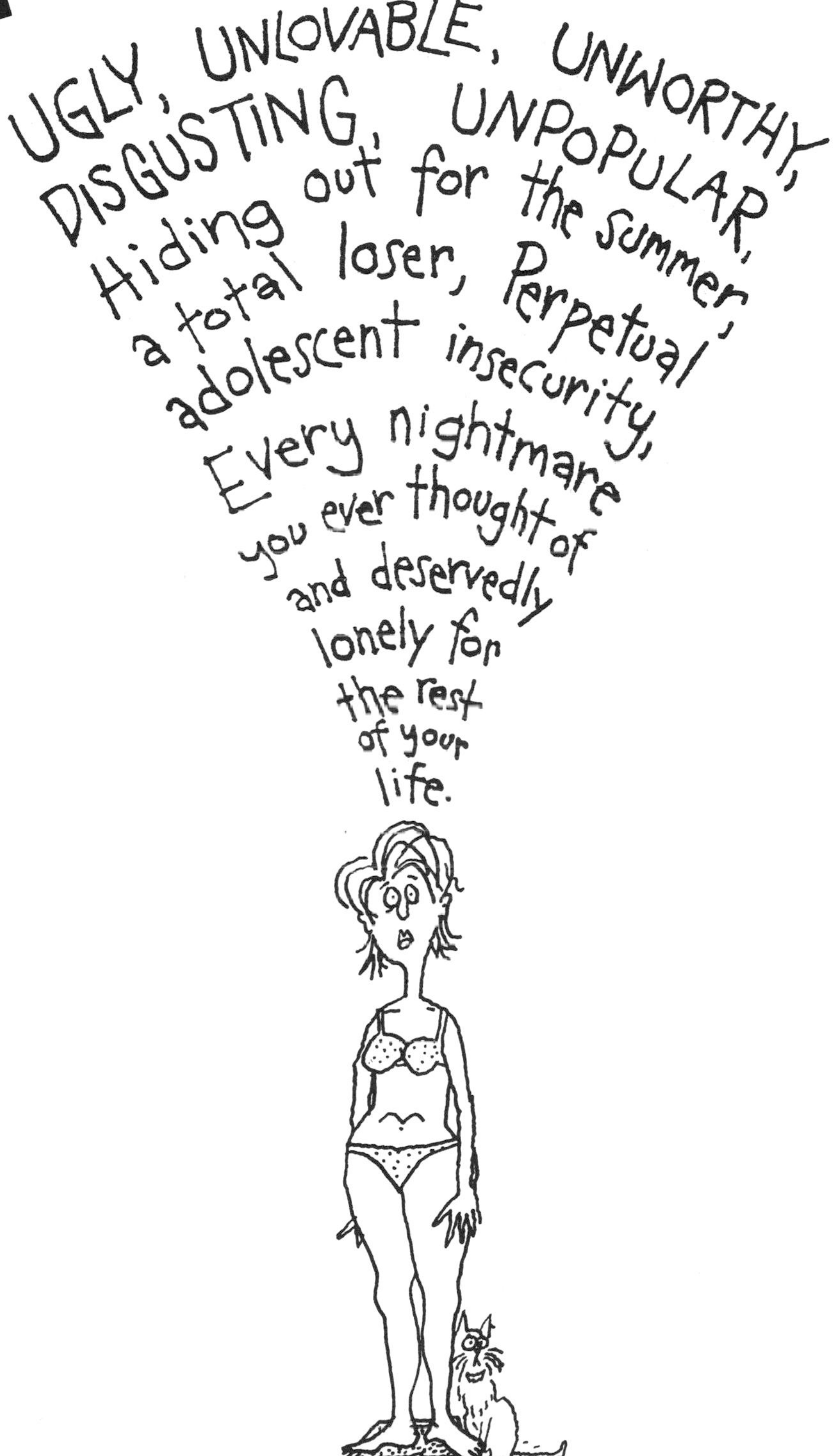
UGLY, UNLOVABLE, UNWORTHY, DISGUSTING, UNPOPULAR, Hiding out for the summer, a total loser, Perpetual adolescent insecurity, Every nightmare you ever thought of and deservedly lonely for the rest of your life.

HOW TO DEAL WITH EXCESS OIL

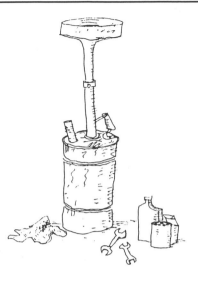

Step 1

Assemble the proper tools

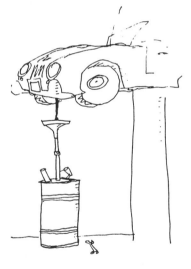

Step 2

Drain appropriately

Step 3

Make sure the area is clean

Step 1

Assemble the
proper tools

Step 2

Drain appropriately

Step 3

Make sure the area is clean

continued

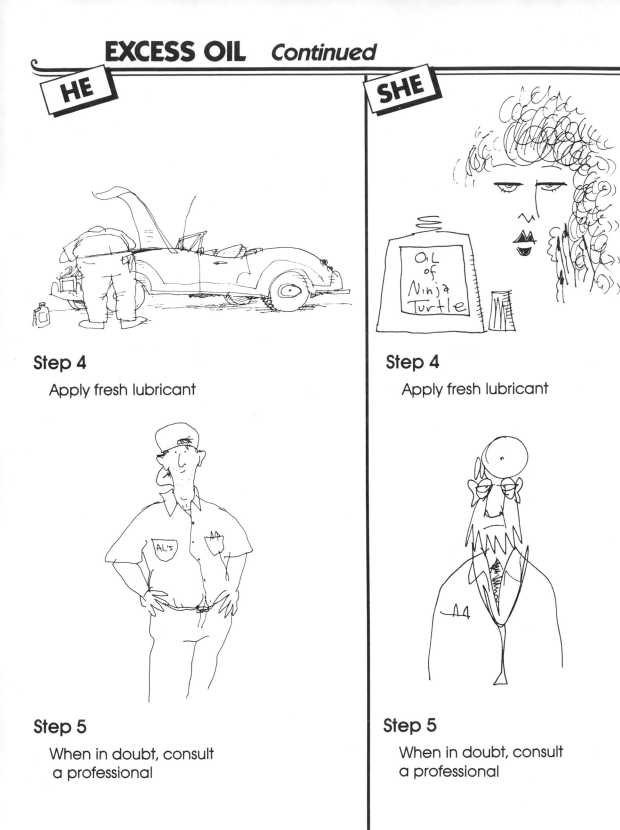

EXCESS OIL *Continued*

HE

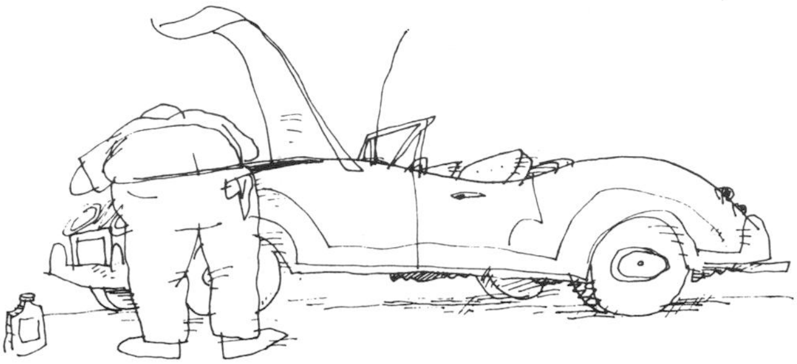

Step 4

Apply fresh lubricant

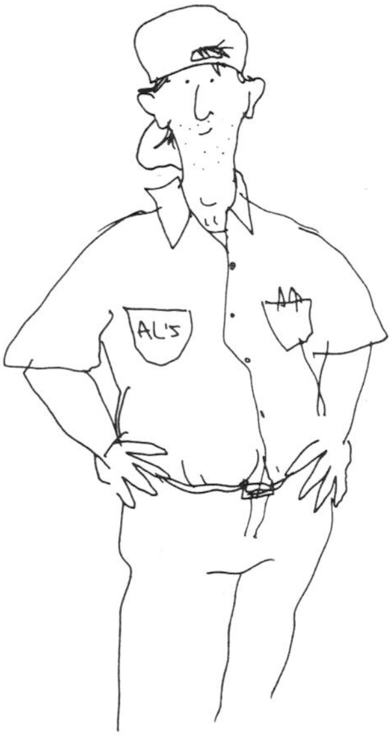
AL'S

Step 5

When in doubt, consult a professional

SHE

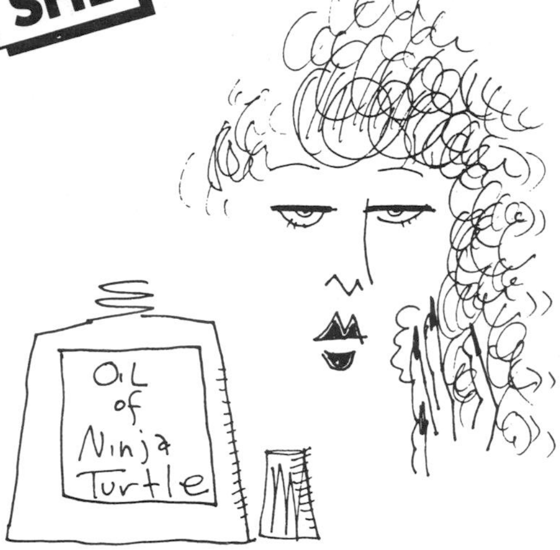
OiL
of
Ninja
Turtle

Step 4

Apply fresh lubricant

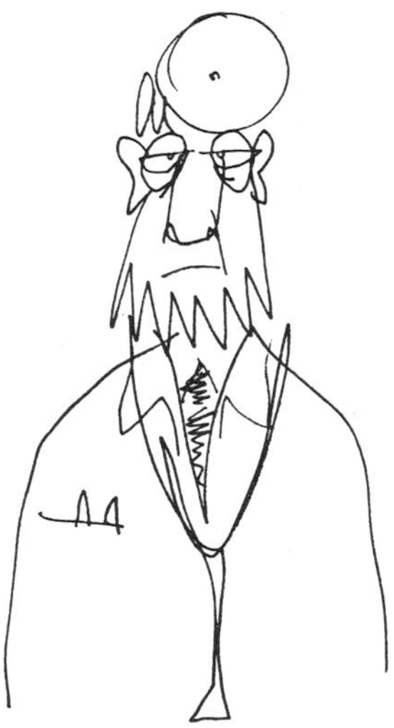

Step 5

When in doubt, consult a professional

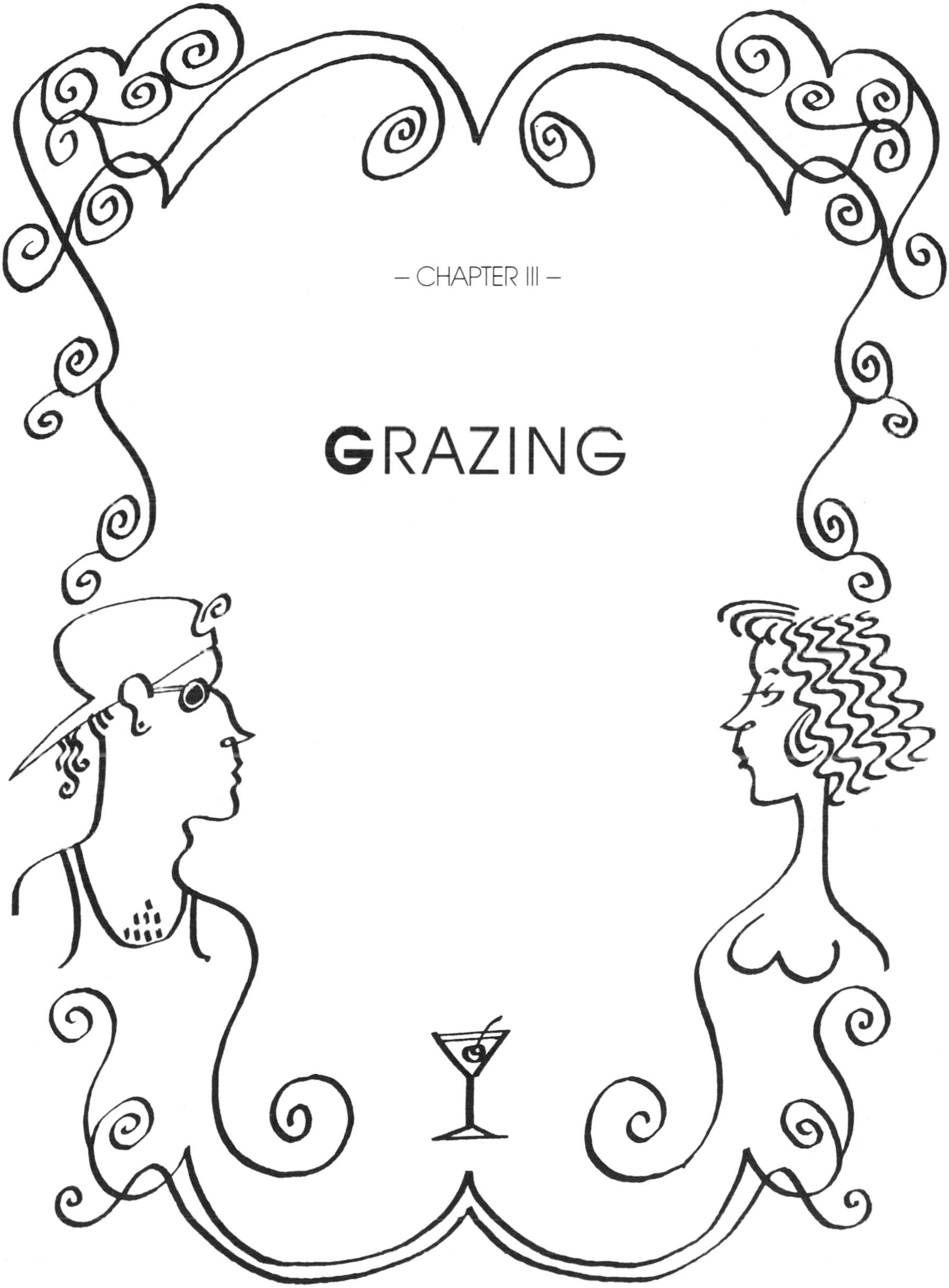

– CHAPTER III –

GRAZING

THE MEANING OF MEALS

HE

When HE Asks Her Out For	*It Means*
Lunch 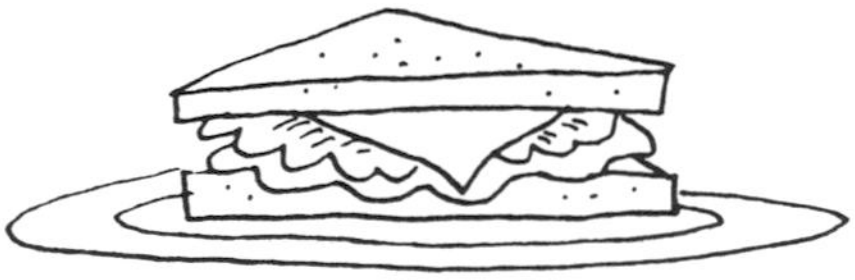	"I might want to sleep with you."
Dinner 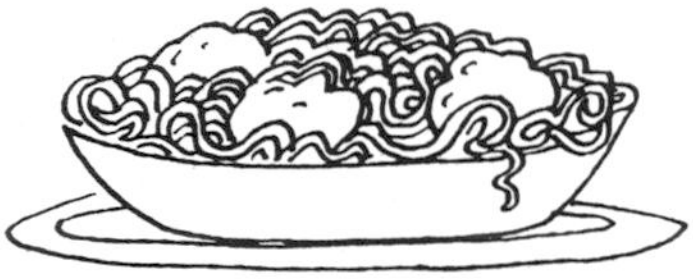	"I want to sleep with you."
Drinks 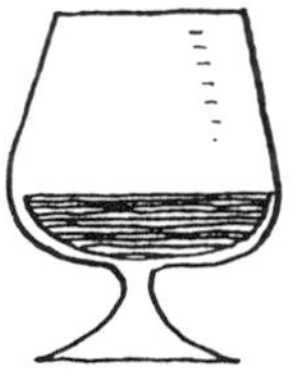	"I want to sleep with you but with no strings attached."
Coffee 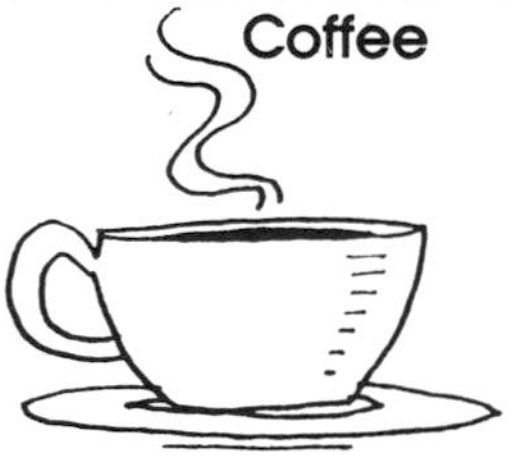	"I want to sleep with you . . . in about an hour."
Breakfast 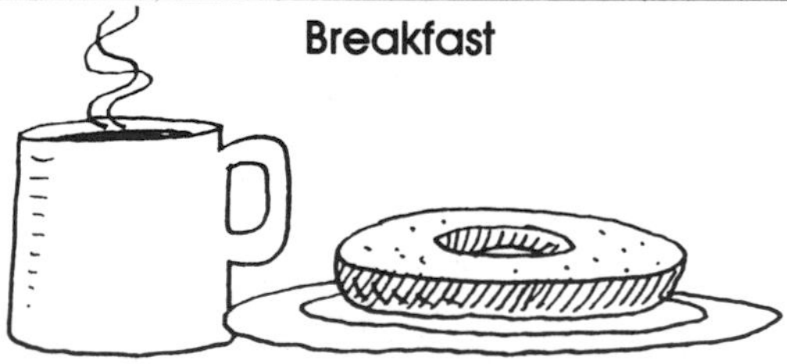	"I already slept with you."
High tea 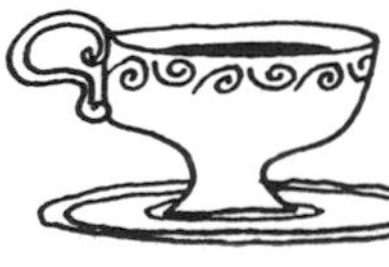	"I'm gay and I don't want to sleep with you."

SHE

When SHE Accepts	*It Means*
Lunch 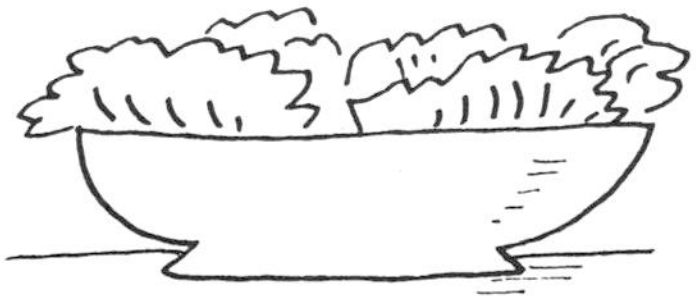	"I might consider having dinner with you."
Dinner 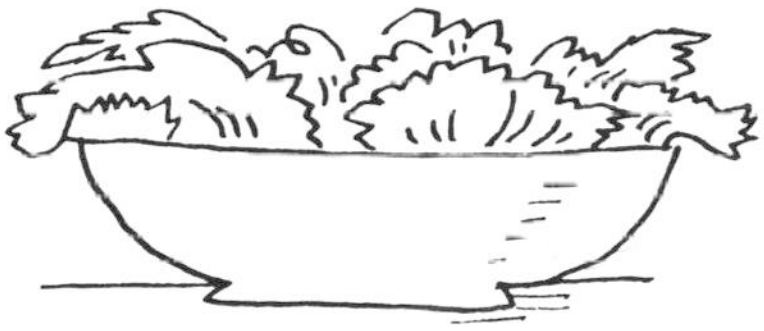	"I might consider sleeping with you."
Drinks 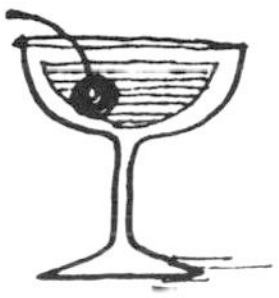	"I'm game."
Coffee 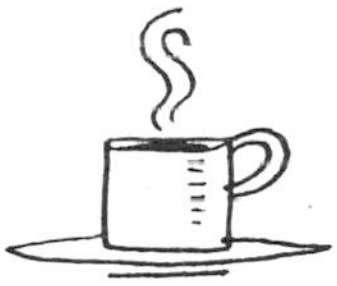	"Let's talk."
Breakfast 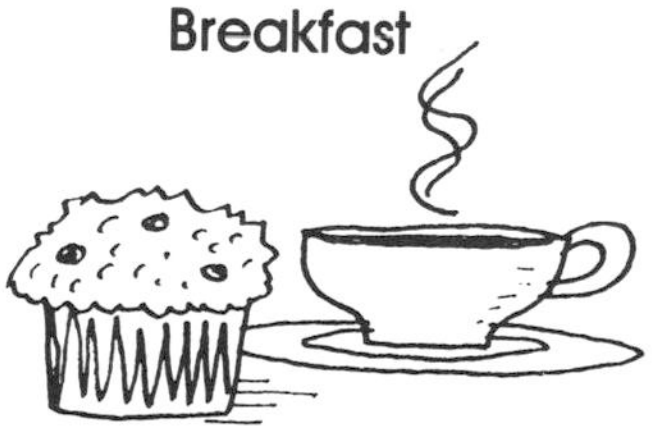	"I want to be like this . . . with you . . . forever."
High tea 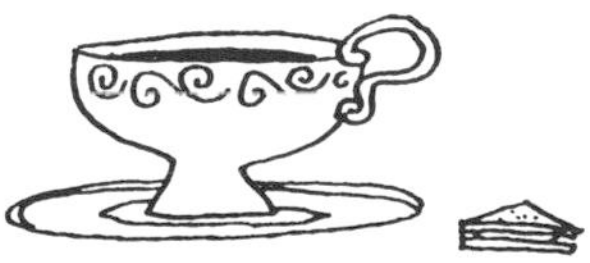	"Well, at least somebody good-looking is taking me out."

REFRIGERATION

HE

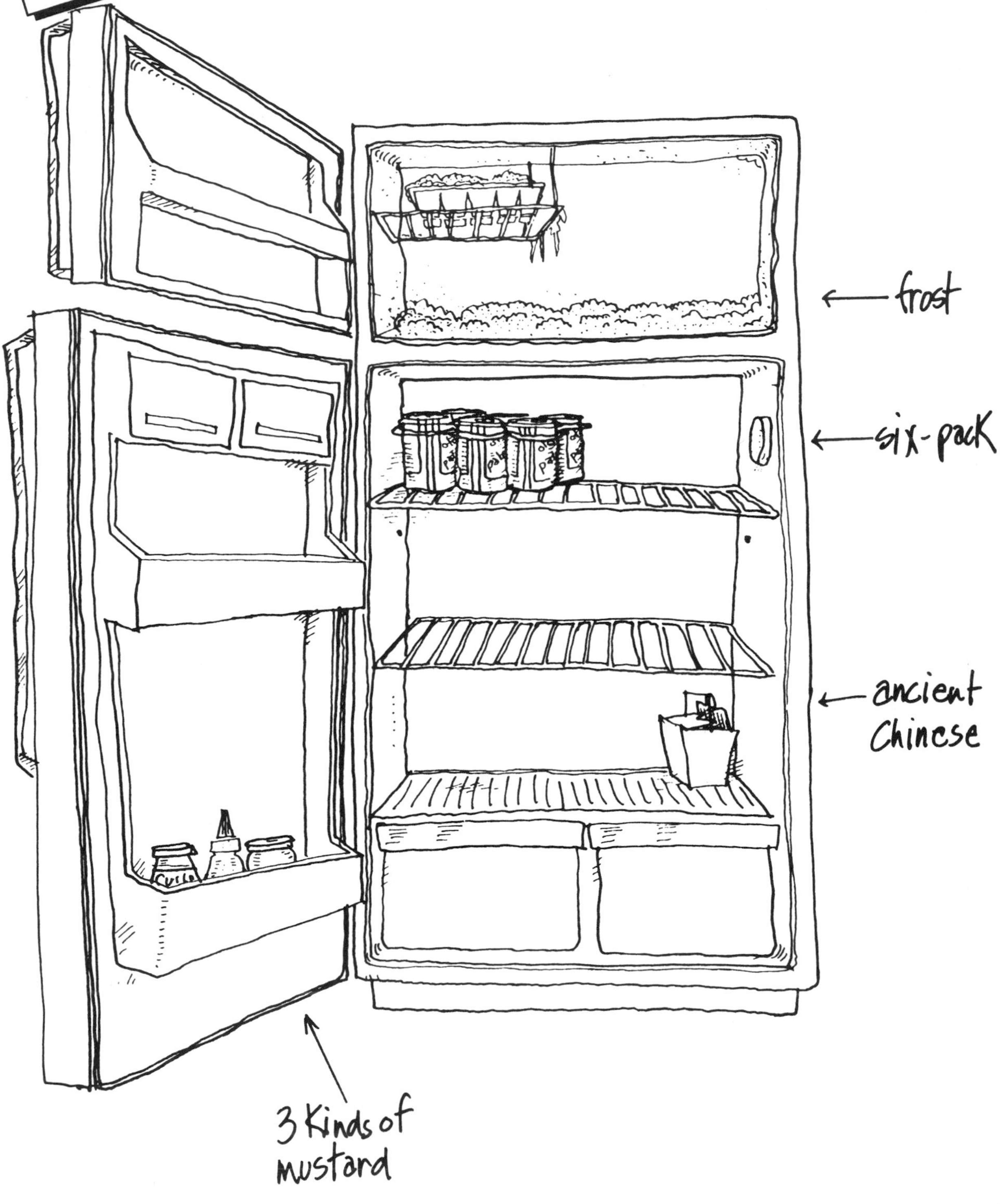

frost
six-pack
ancient Chinese
3 Kinds of mustard

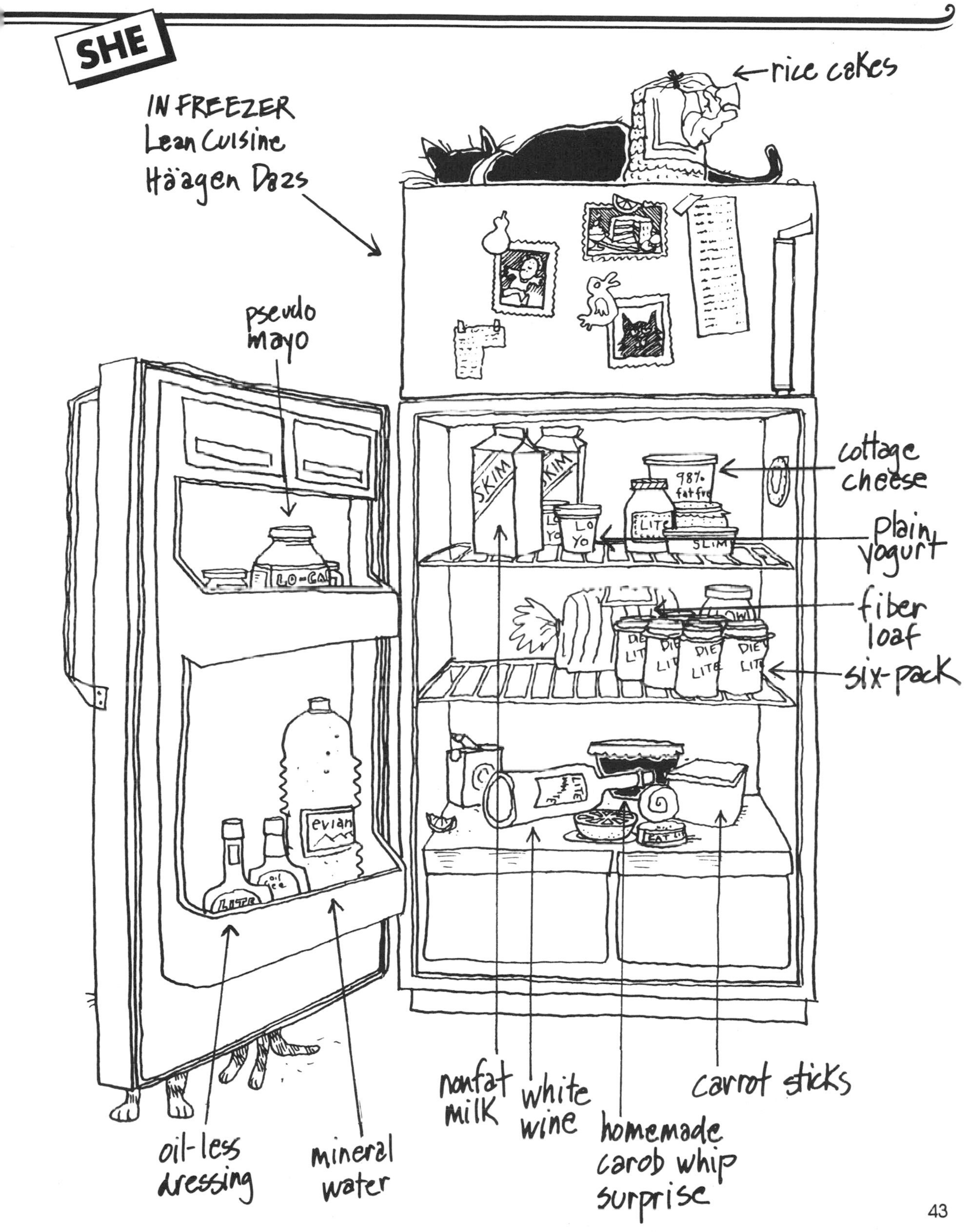
SHE
rice cakes
IN FREEZER
Lean Cuisine
Häagen Dazs
pseudo
mayo
LO-CAL
cottage
cheese
98%
fat fre
SKIM
LO
YO
LITE
SLIM
plain
yogurt
fiber
loaf
DIET
LITE
six-pack
evian
LITE
nonfat
milk
white
wine
homemade
carob whip
surprise
carrot sticks
oil-less
dressing
mineral
water

THE MEANING OF BEER

HE

figure A
guy with beer

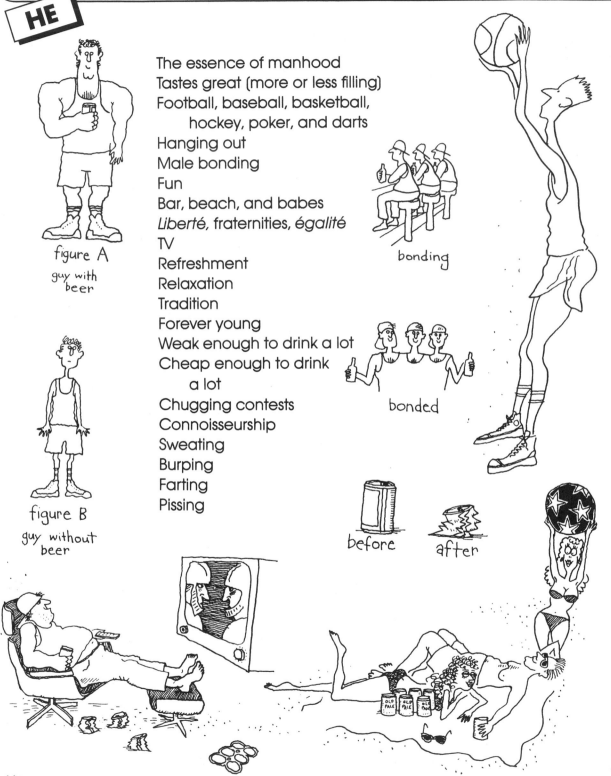

The essence of manhood
Tastes great (more or less filling)
Football, baseball, basketball,
hockey, poker, and darts
Hanging out
Male bonding
Fun
Bar, beach, and babes
Liberté, fraternities, *égalité*
TV
Refreshment
Relaxation
Tradition
Forever young
Weak enough to drink a lot
Cheap enough to drink
a lot
Chugging contests
Connoisseurship
Sweating
Burping
Farting
Pissing

bonding

bonded

figure B
guy without beer

before

after

OLD PALE
OLD PALE
OLD PALE

Liquid bread

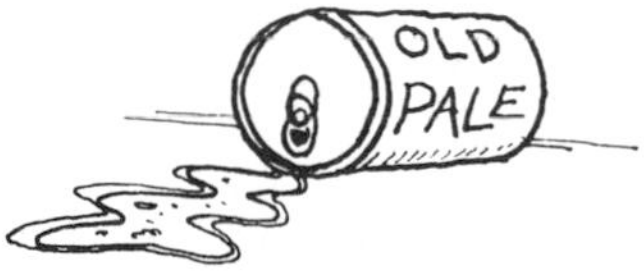
OLD
PALE

HE

ON A DIET

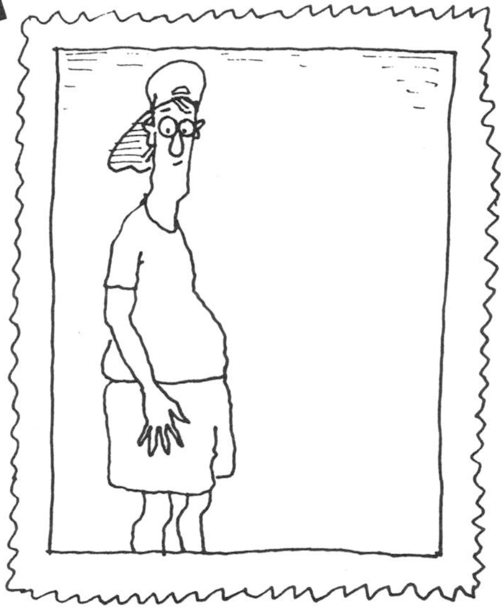

Before

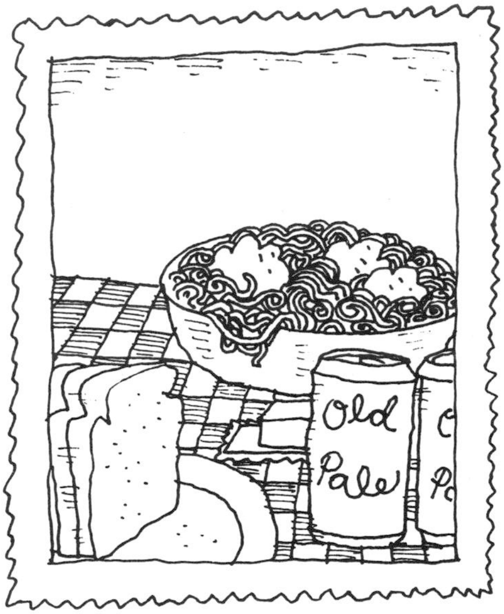
Old
Pale

The Regime

1) Skip third piece of bread at dinner
2) Cut down on alcohol

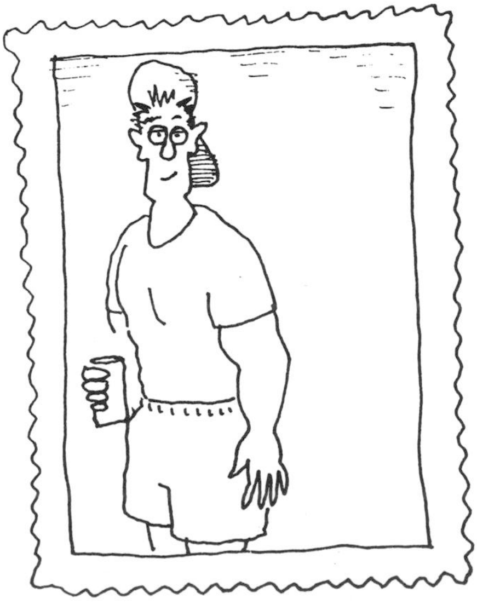

After two weeks,
total weight loss: 8 lbs.

Before

continued

ON A DIET *Continued*

SHE

The Regime

1) No-fat, high-fiber, 600-calorie diet

The Grapefruit Diet

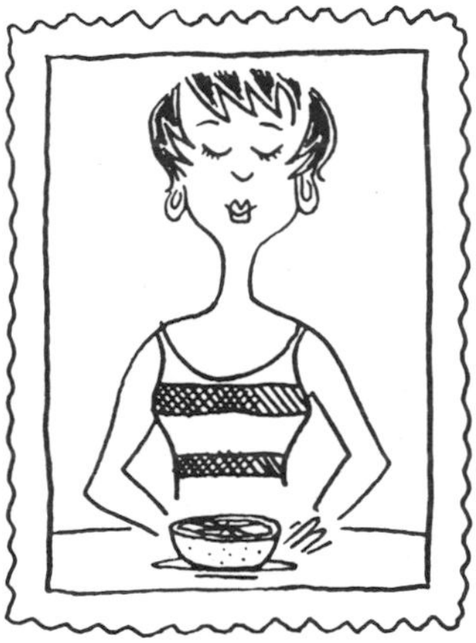

First month

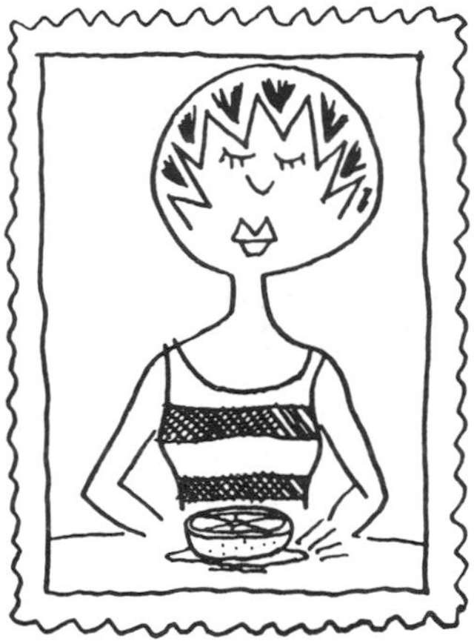

Second month

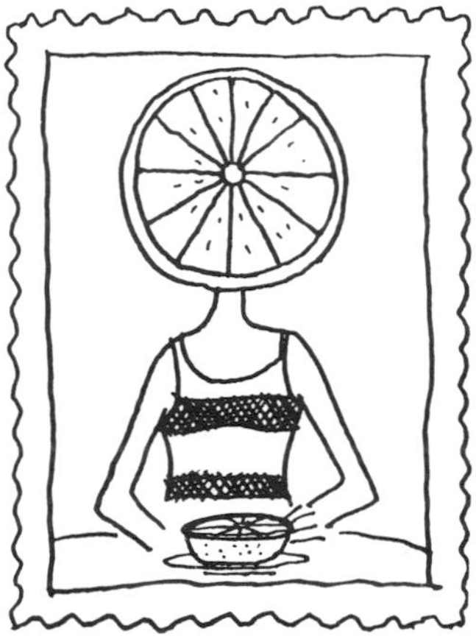

Third month

2) 32 glasses of water a day

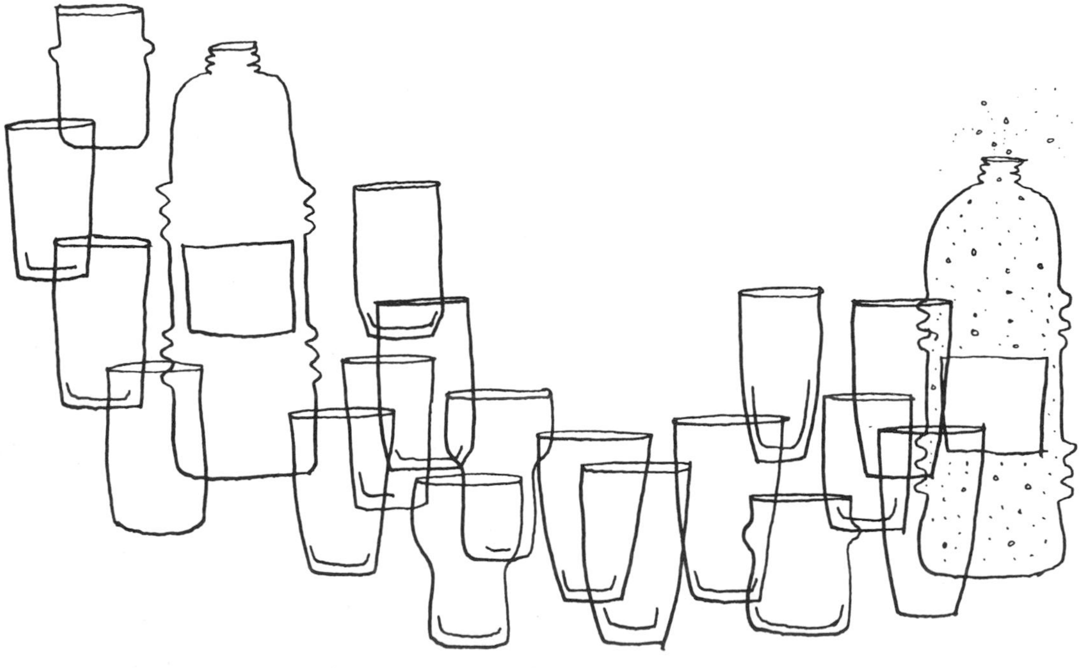

Reward System

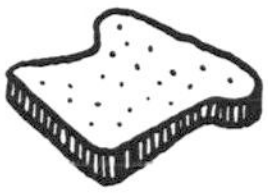		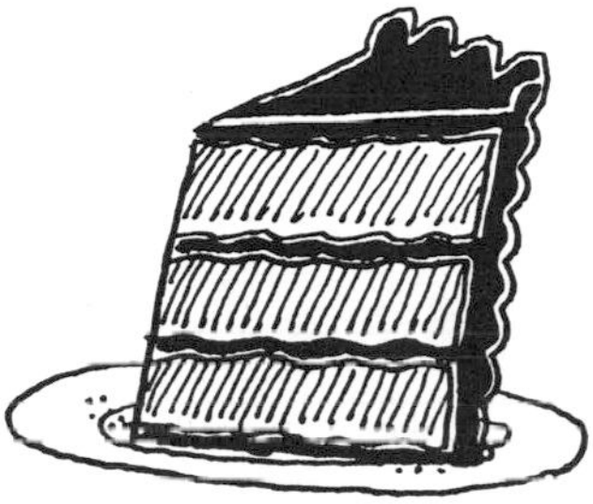
Real bread (once a week)	Pat of butter (once per annum)	Chocolate cake (when hell freezes over)

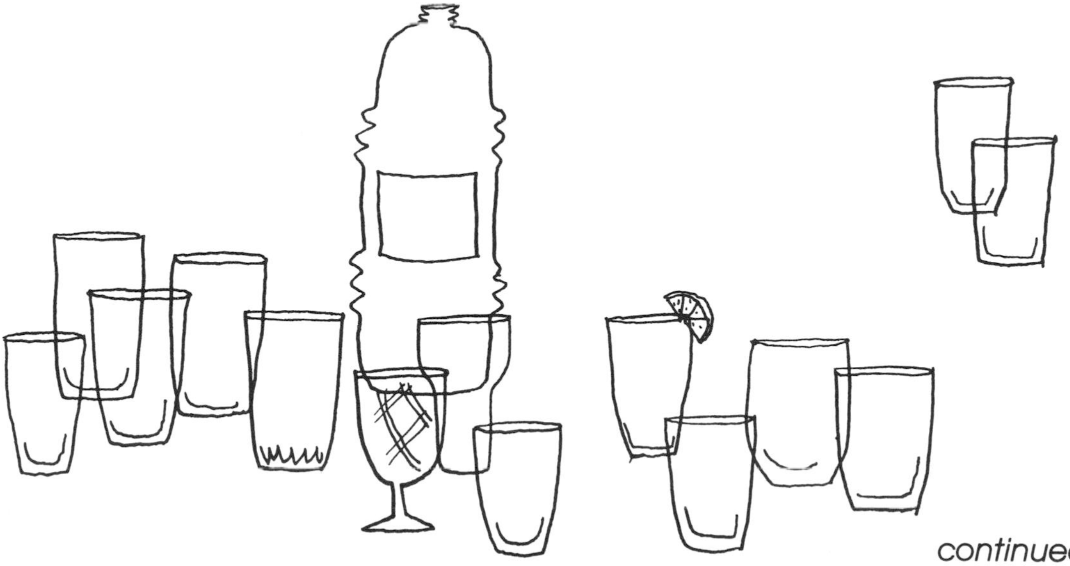

continued

SHE

3) Jog 7 miles/5 days a week

4) Low impact/twice a day,
   every day

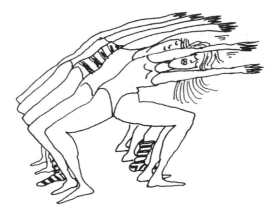

5) Karen's killer step
   class/3 times a week

6) Every day/45 minutes

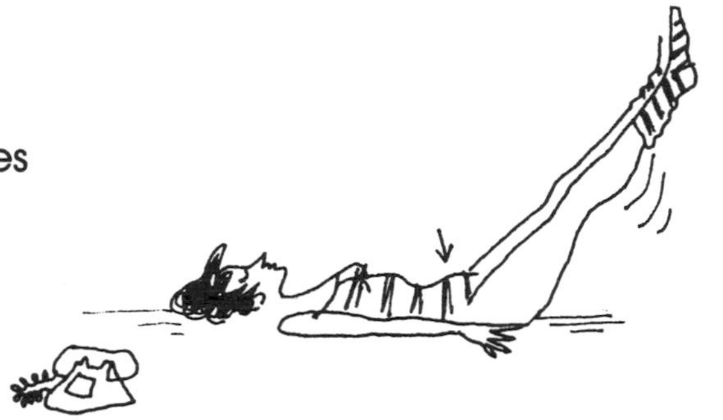

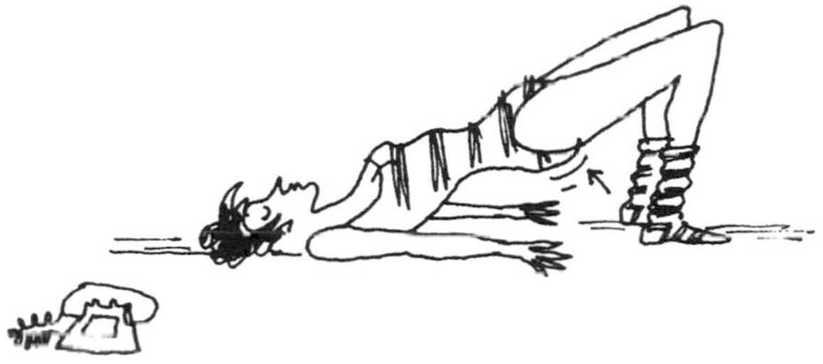

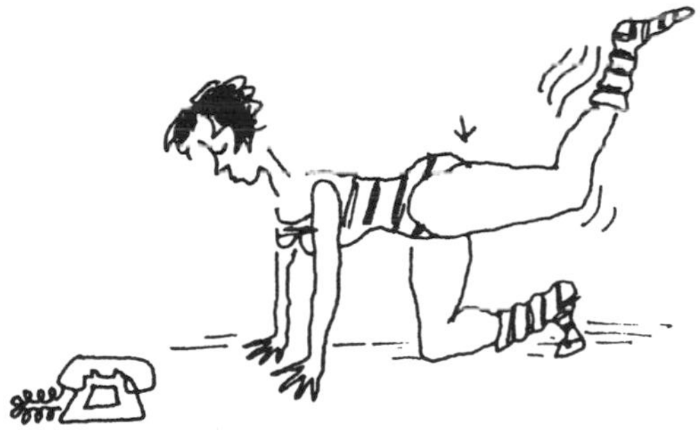

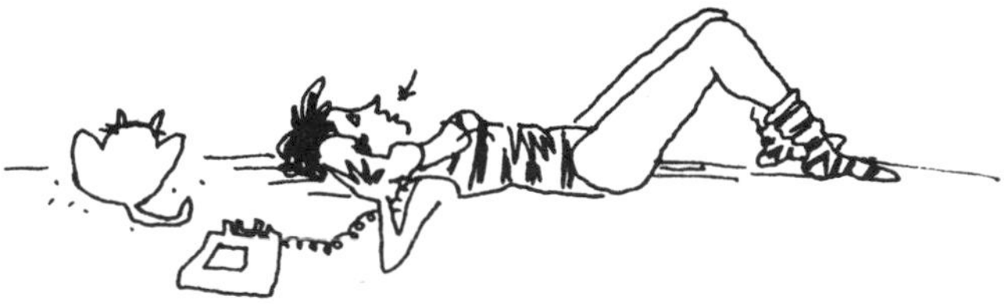

continued

After three months,
total weight loss: 6½ oz.

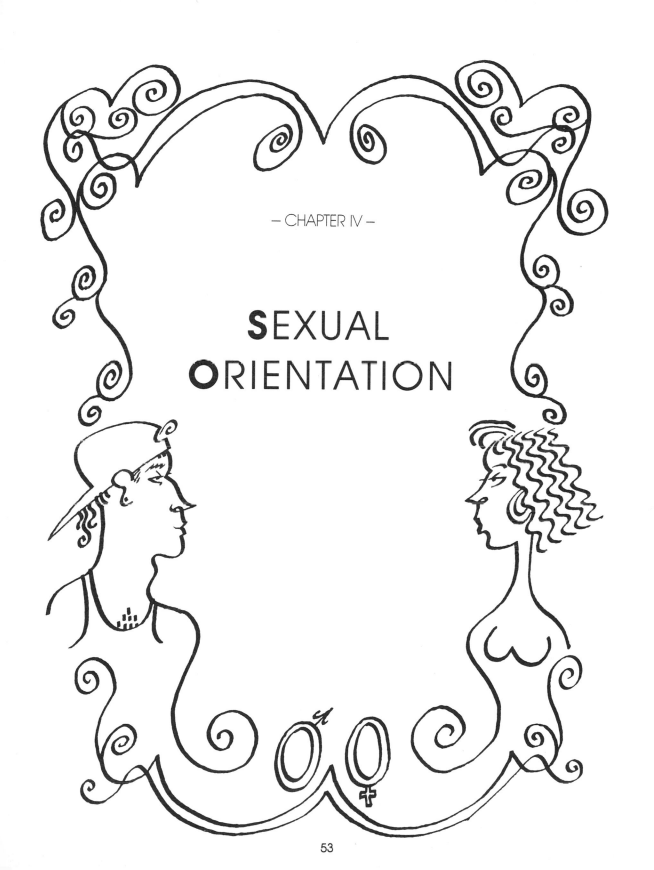

– CHAPTER IV –

SEXUAL ORIENTATION

SEXUAL PREFERENCES

HE

He dreams of sex in general . . .

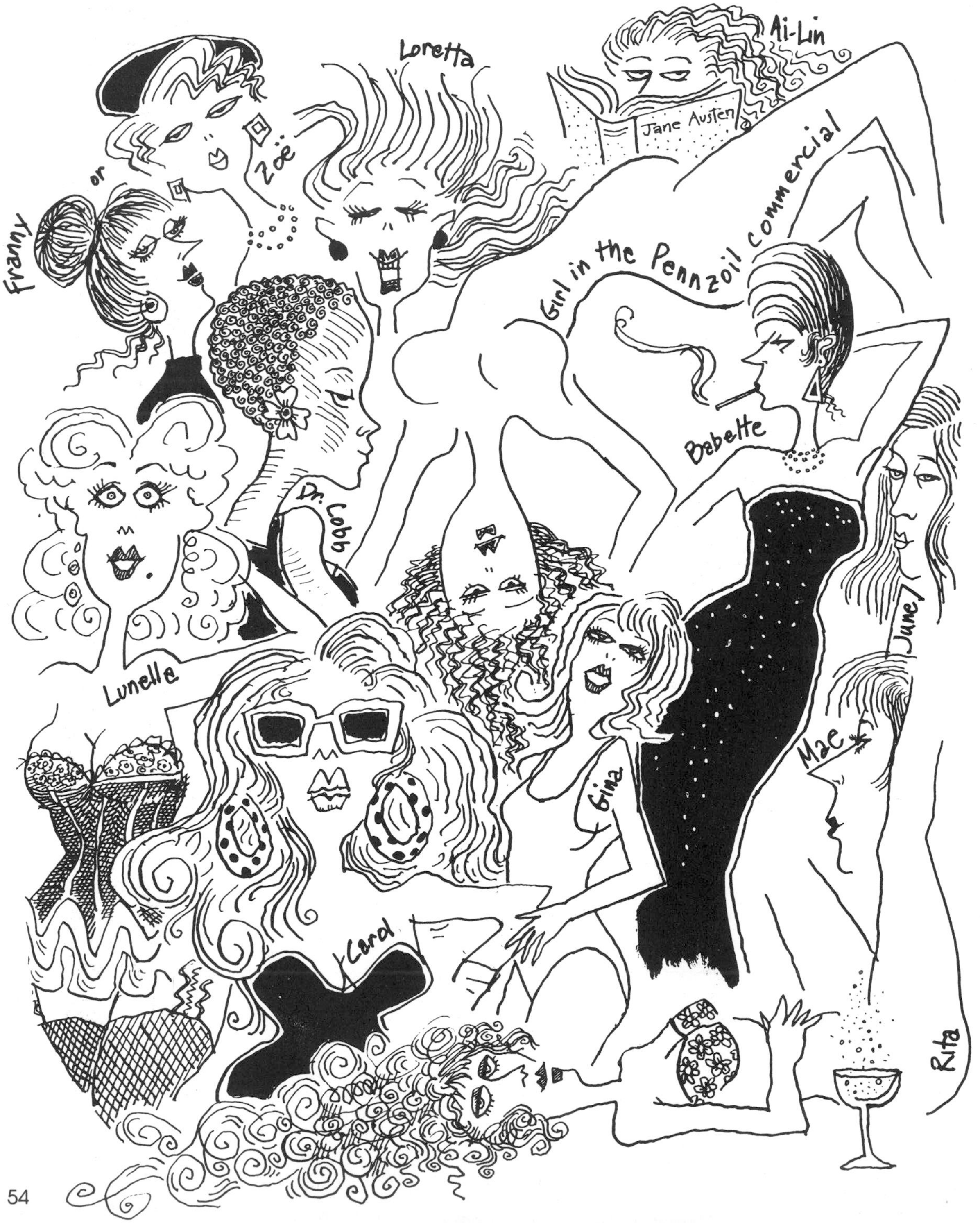

Loretta
Ai-Lin
Jane Austen
Zoë
or
Franny
Girl in the Pennzoil commercial
Babette
Dr. Cobb
Lunelle
June
Mae
Gina
Carol
Rita

SHE

She dreams of sex in particular . . .

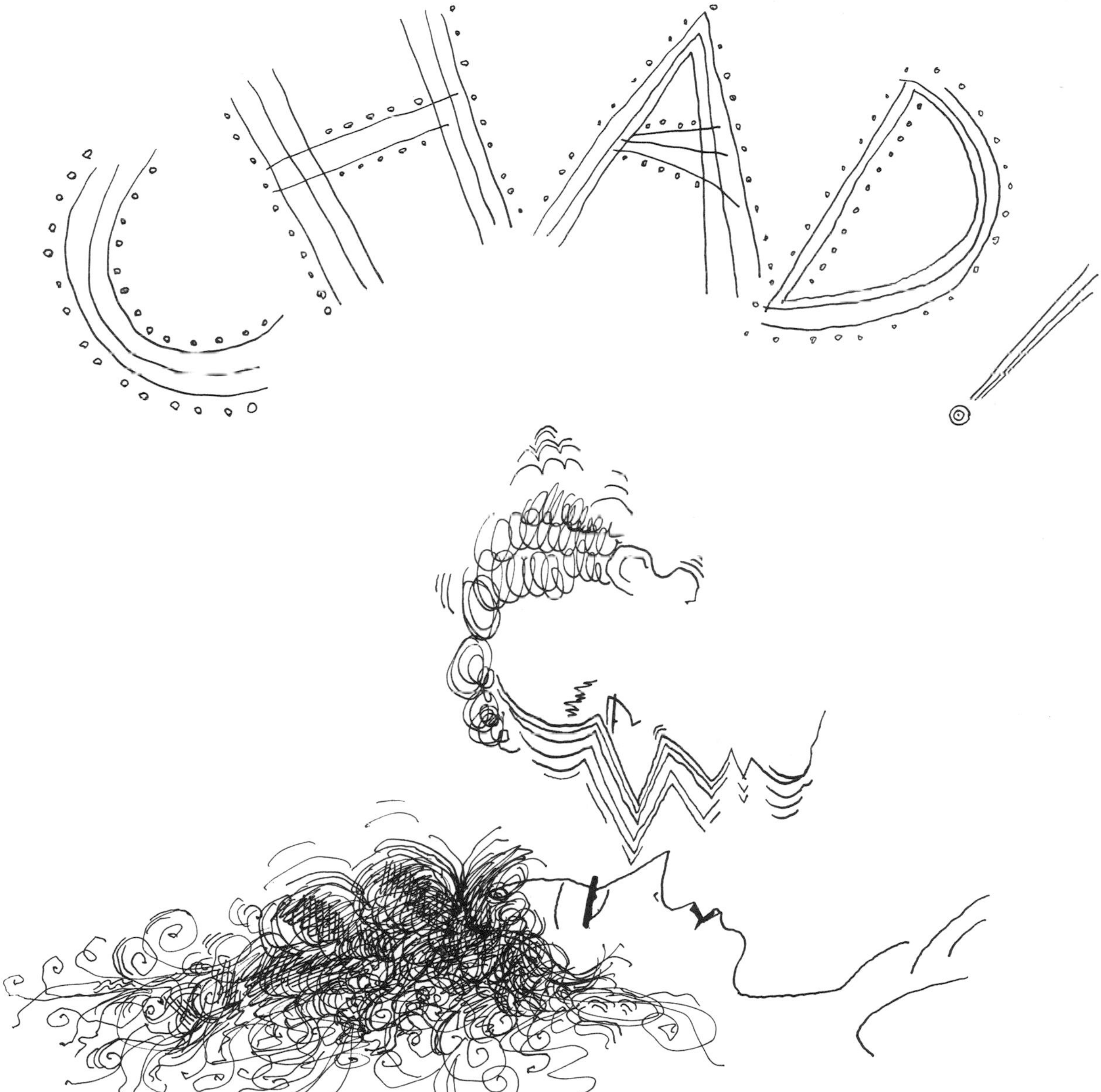
CHAD!

BIOLOGICAL CLOCKS

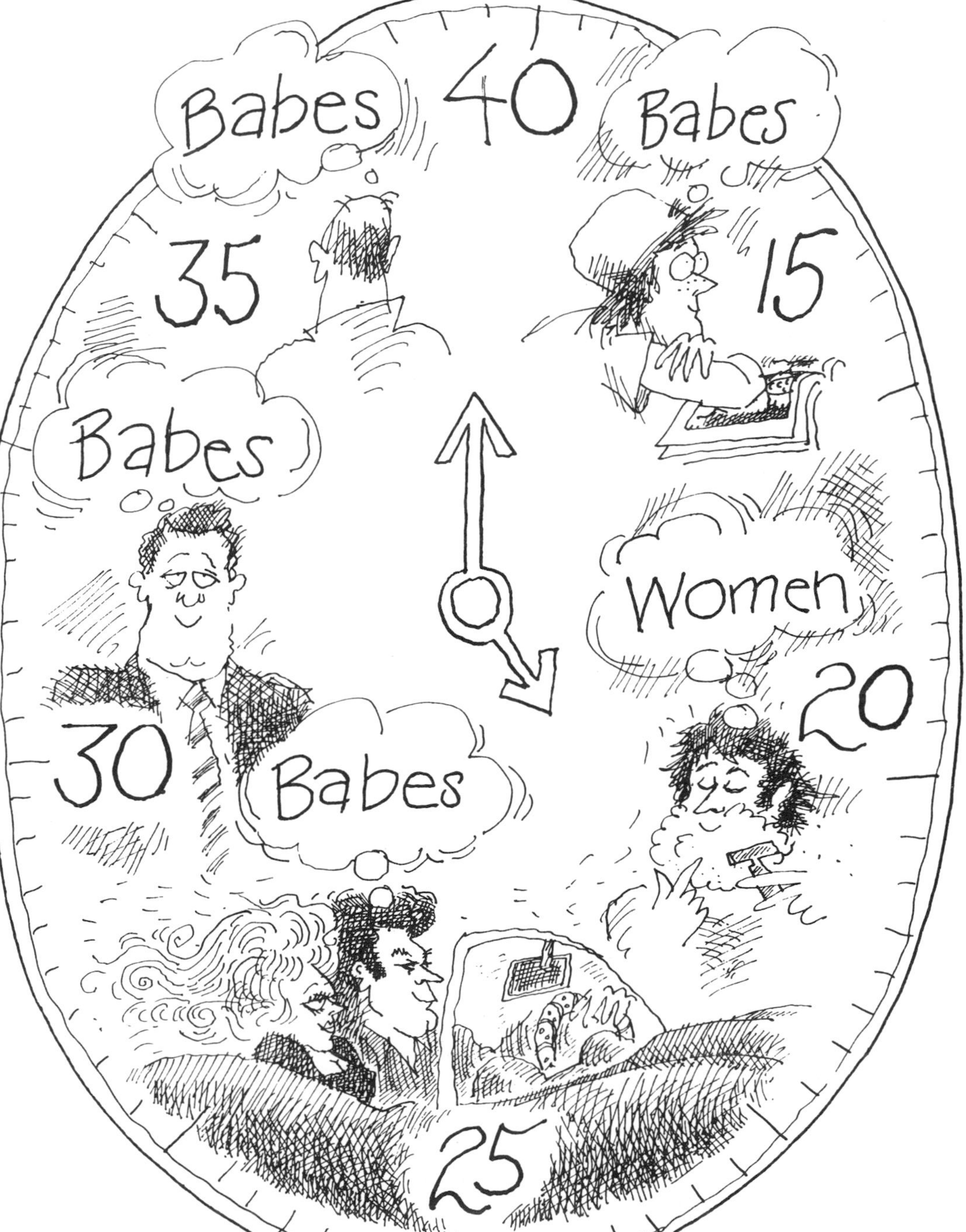
40
Babes
Babes
35
15
Babes
Women
20
30
Babes
25

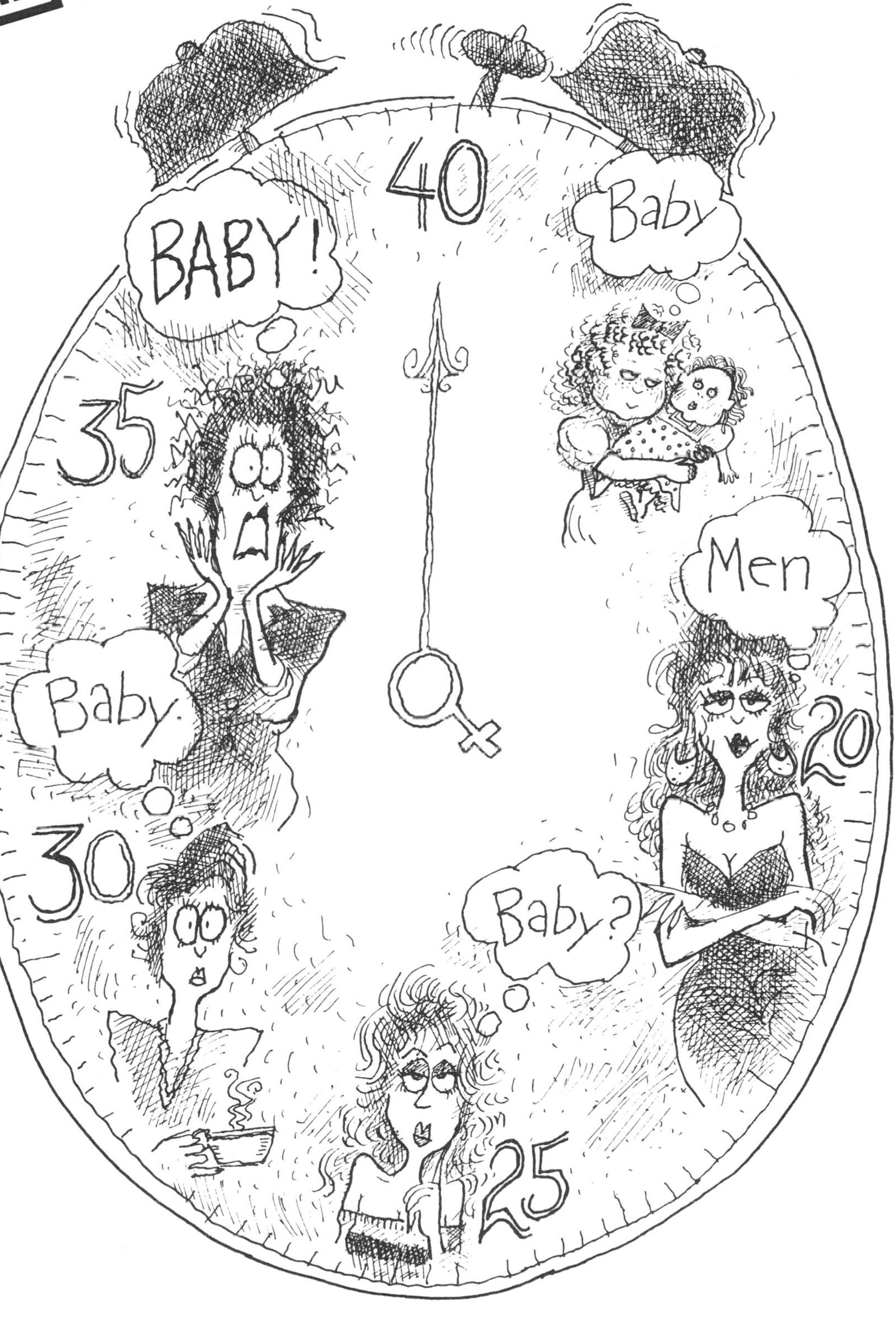
40
Baby
BABY!
35
Men
Baby
20
30
Baby?
25

THE PERFECT DAY

HE

10:00 Wake up

10:02 Oral sex

10:20 Shower

10:45 Big breakfast

11:30 Drive up coast in Ferrari Testarossa with outrageous blonde

P.M.

2:15 Enormous lunch

3:00 Oral sex in the sand

3:30 Sports with the guys

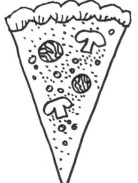

58

SHE

A.M. **8:45** Wake up thin

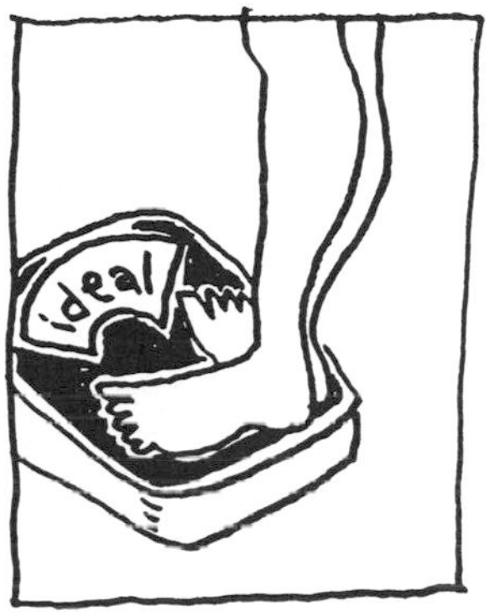
ideal

8:50 Hugs and kisses

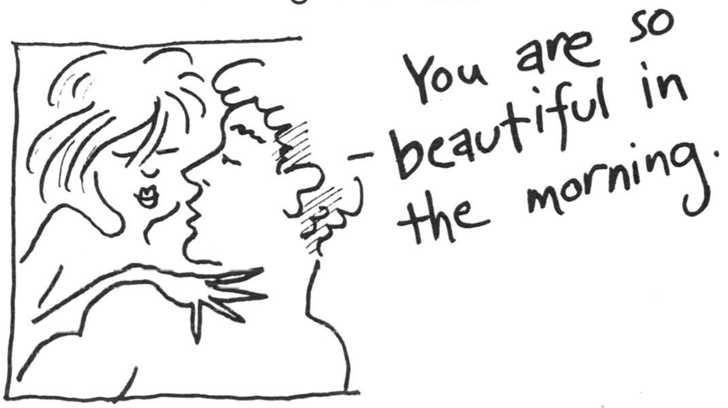
You are so beautiful in the morning.

9:30 Light breakfast

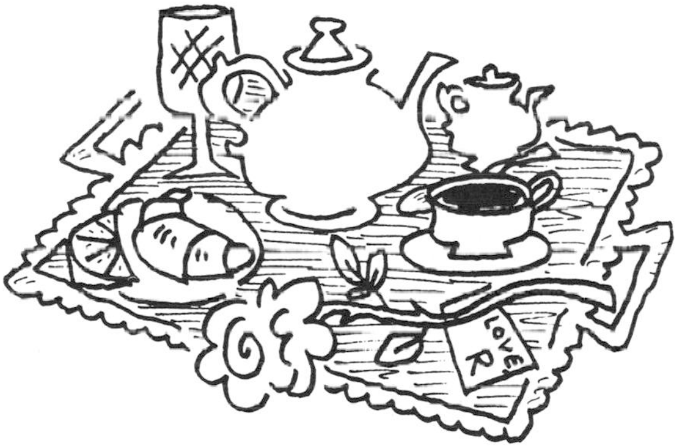
LOVE
R

11:00 Sunbathe

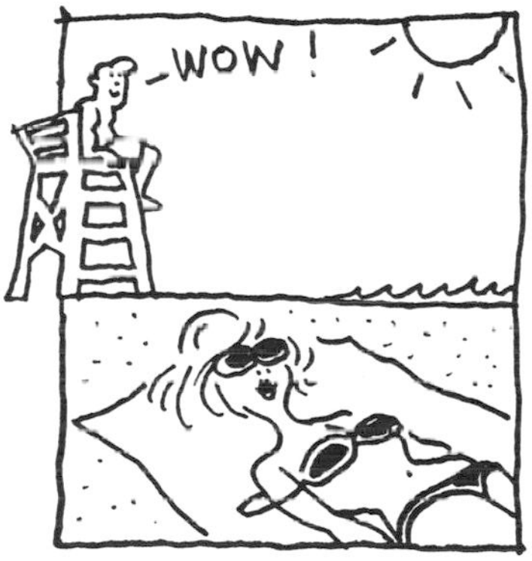
WOW!

P.M. **Noon** Lunch with best friend at an outdoor cafe

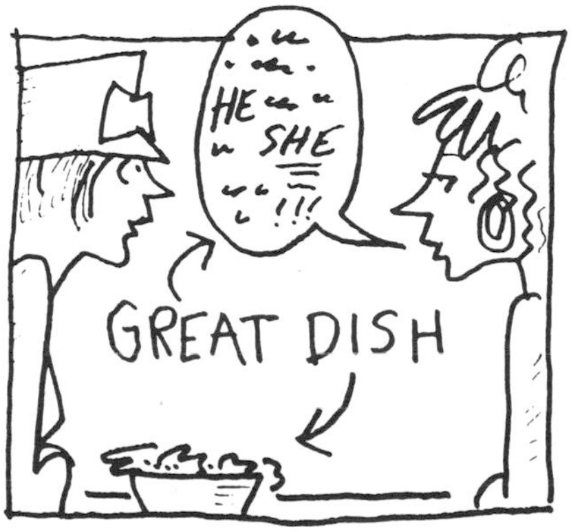
HE
SHE
GREAT DISH

1:30 Shopping

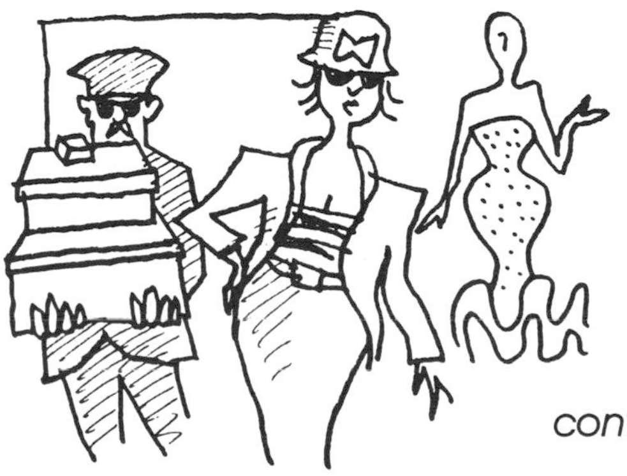

continued

THE PERFECT DAY *Continued*

HE

P.M. **3:31** Drink beer

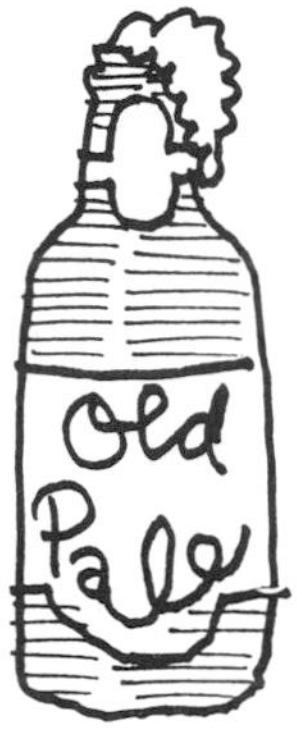
Old Pale

4:30 Hang with the guys at the bar

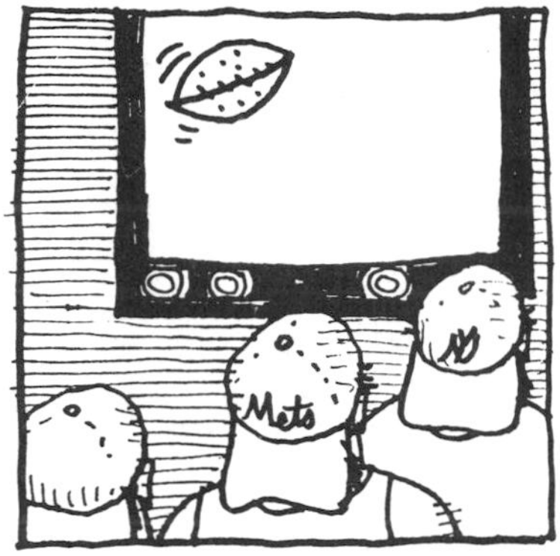
Mets

5:30 Meet Kim Basinger there

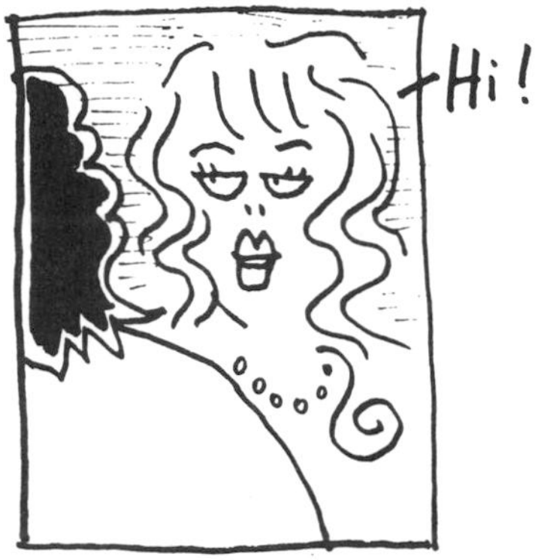
Hi!

5:32 Get her phone number

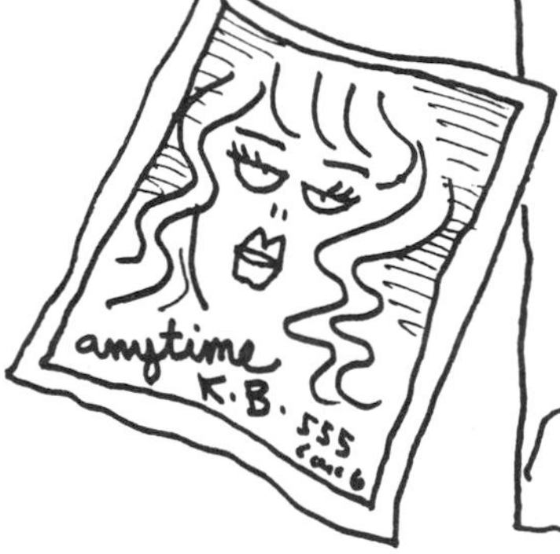
anytime
K.B.
555

5:45 Oral sex

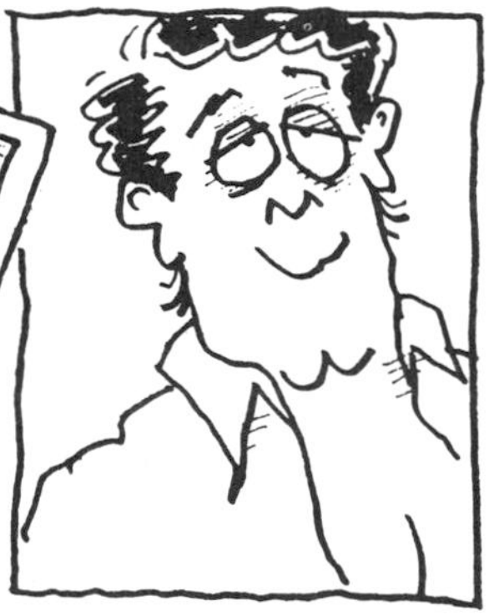

6:00 More beer

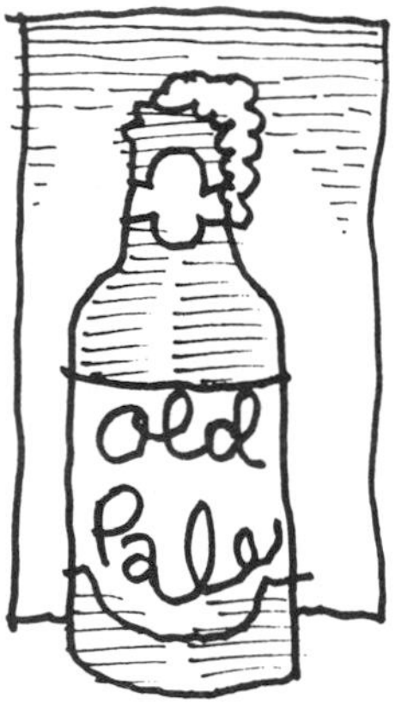
Old Pale

8:00 Huge dinner

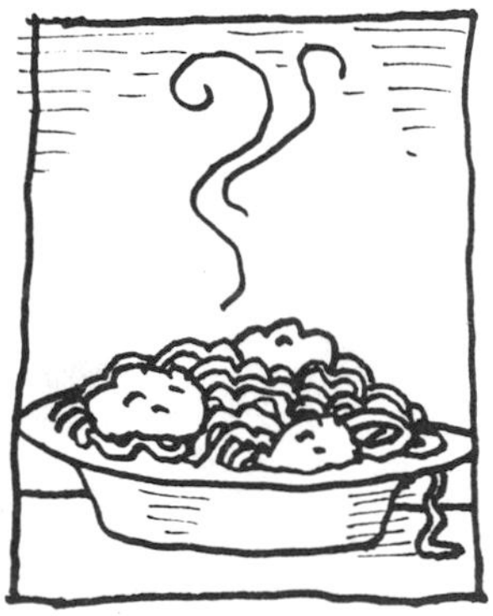

11:00 Full-on, get-down gorilla sex

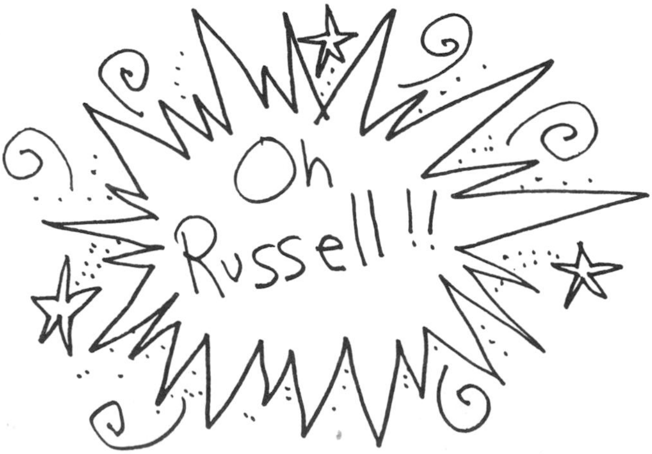
Oh Russell!!

SHE

P.M. **1:45** Run into boyfriend's ex

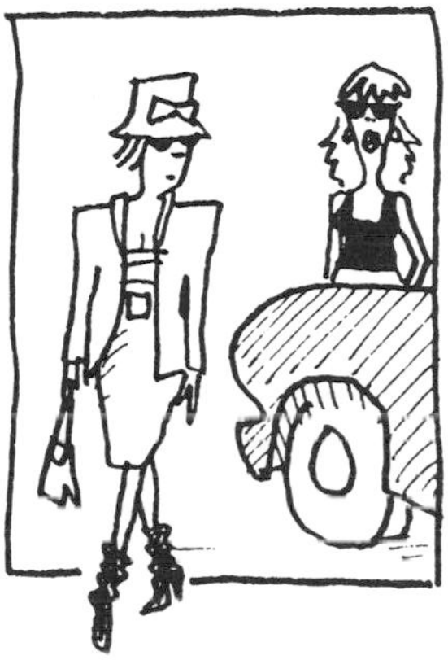

1:46 Notice that she's gained 30 lbs.

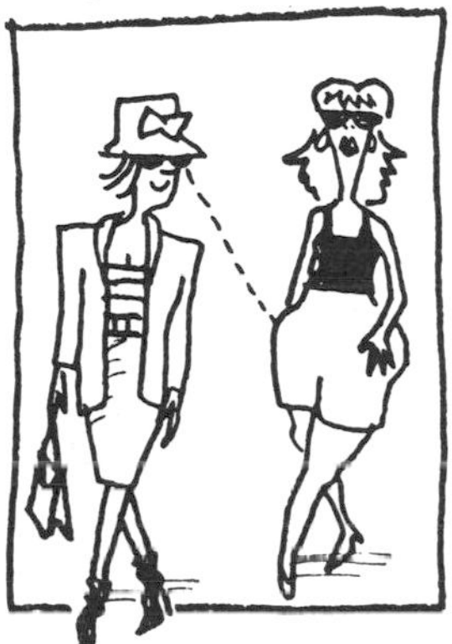

3:00 Facial and massage

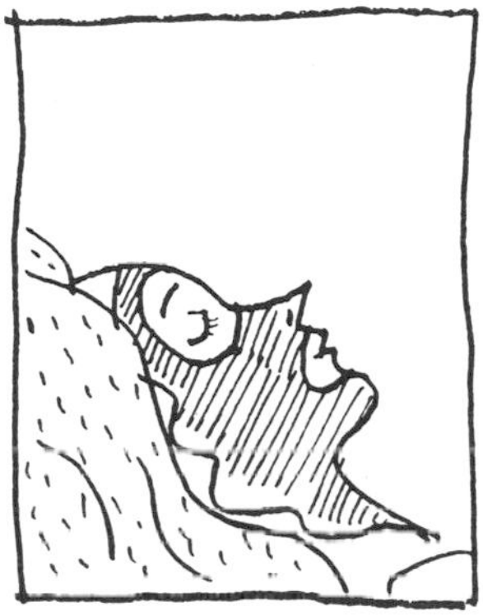

4:30 Nap

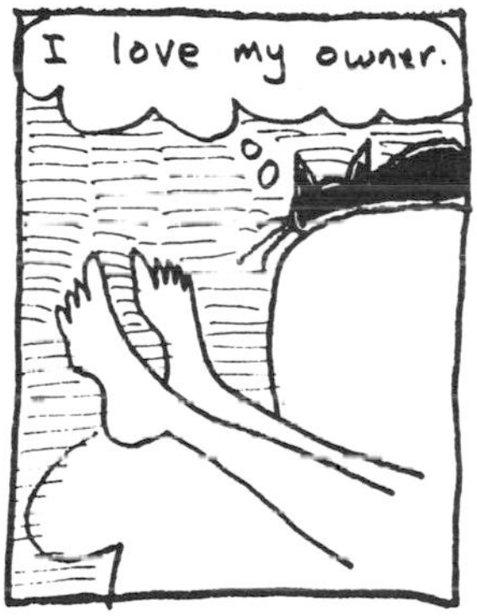
I love my owner.

7:30 Candlelit dinner and dancing à deux

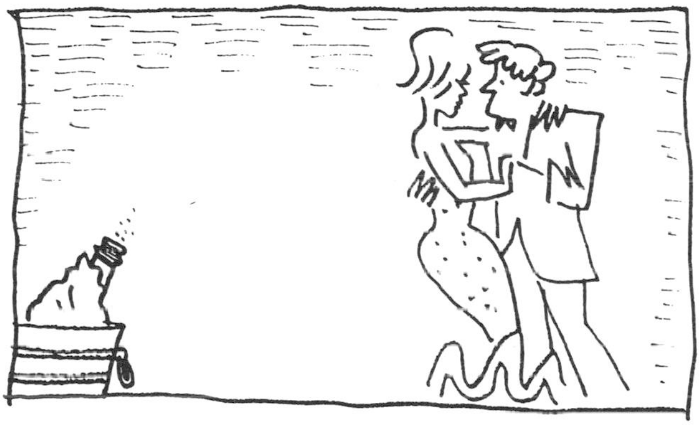

10:00 Make love

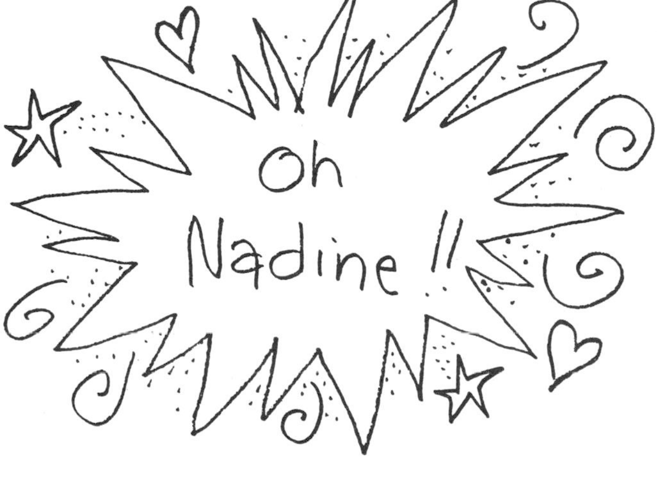
Oh
Nadine!!

11:00 Pillow talk in his big, strong arms

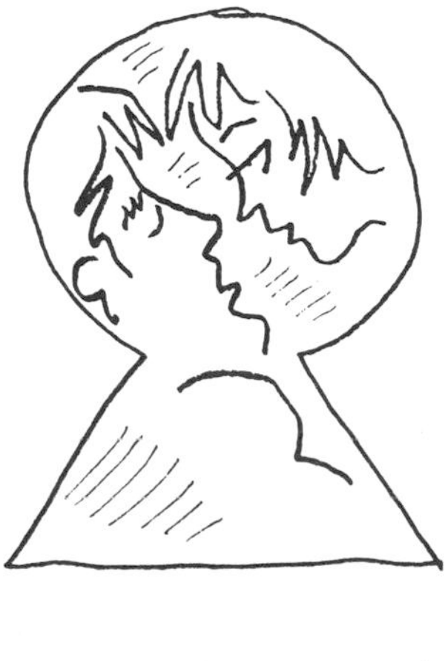

STRANGERS IN PAIN

HE

Pain she will never know:

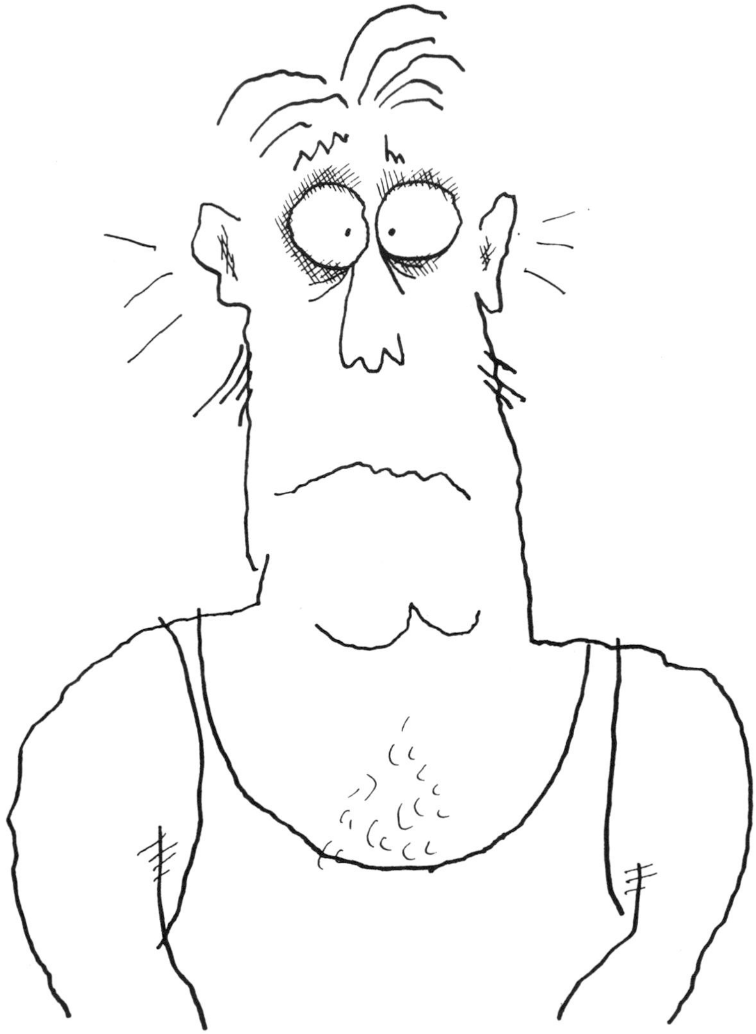

1) Blue balls
2) Swift kick in the groin

Pain he will never know:

1) Cold speculum
2) Menstrual cramps
3) Childbirth
4) Bikini wax

FEAR OF AGING *Kiss the Fantasy Good-bye*

SHE

No more . . .

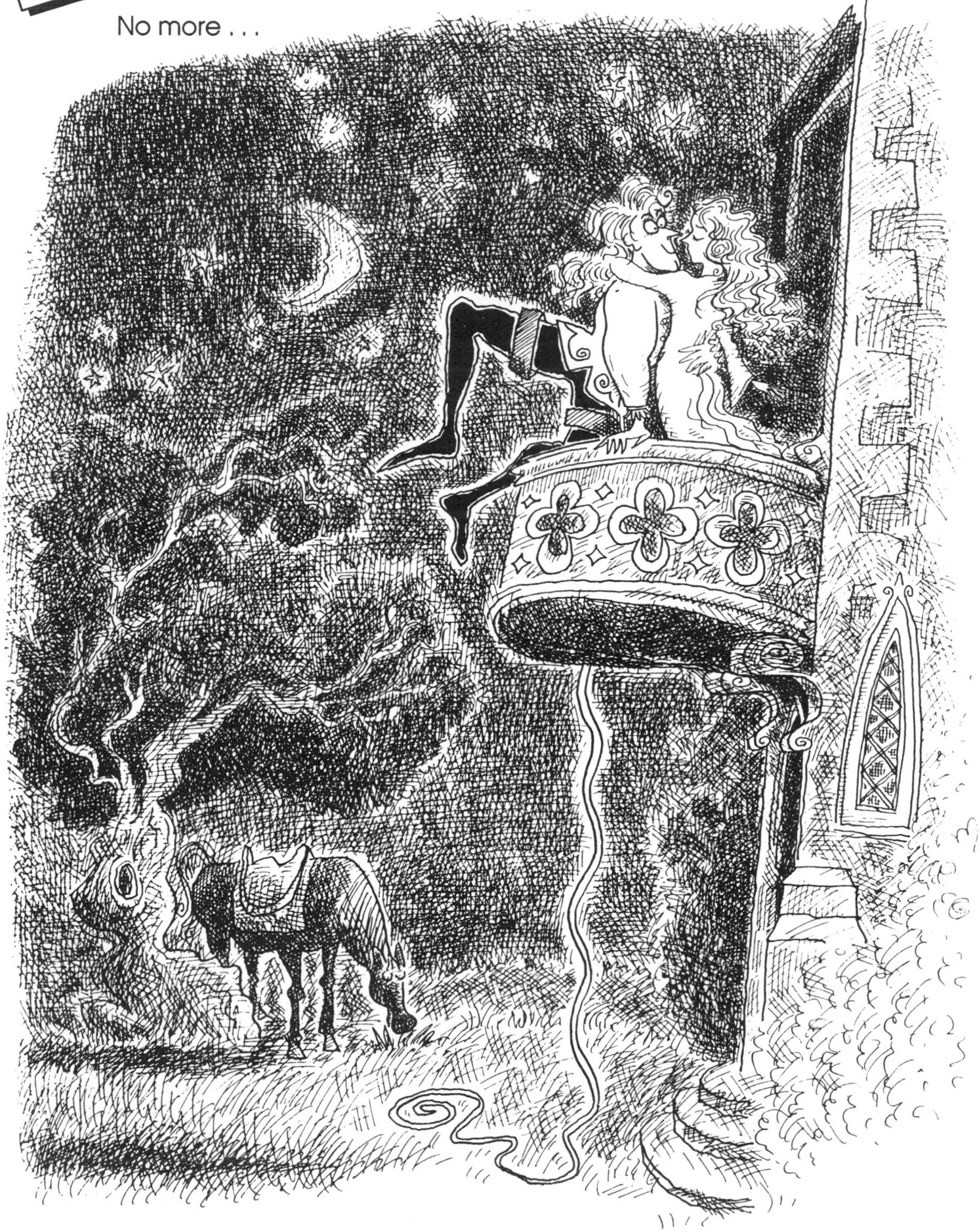

No more . . .

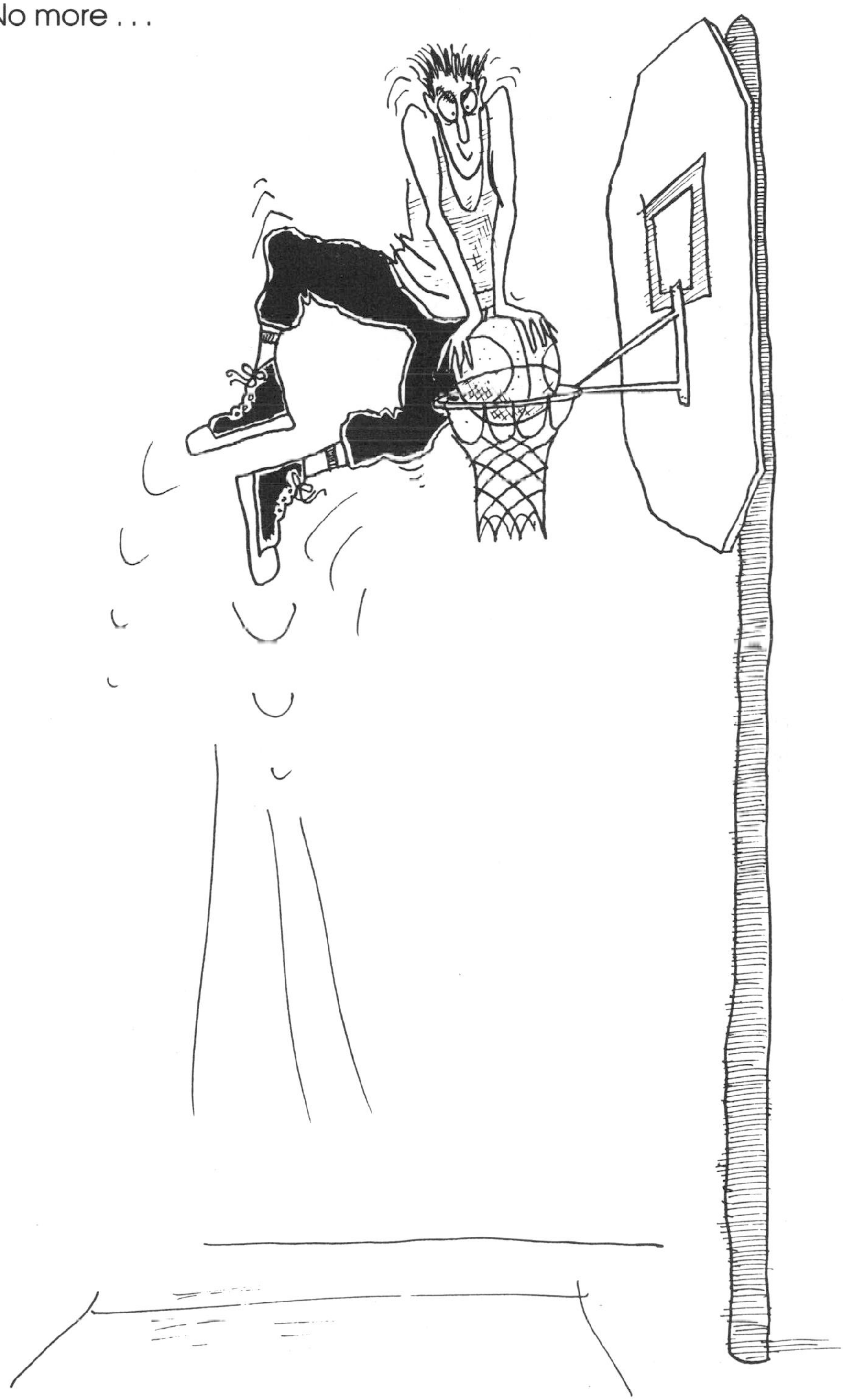

AUTO SUGGESTION

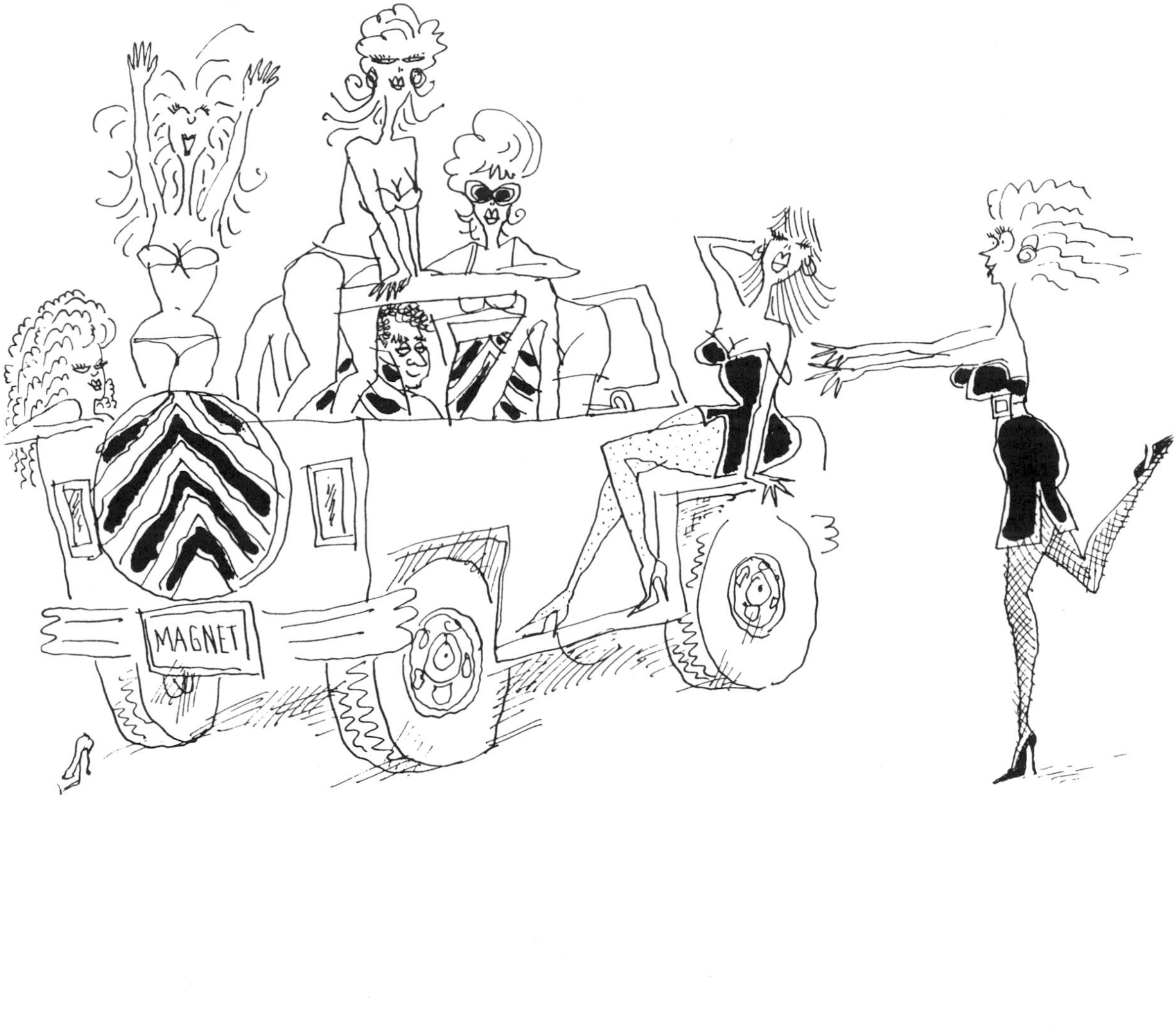
MAGNET

The kind of woman he attracts with a fancy car

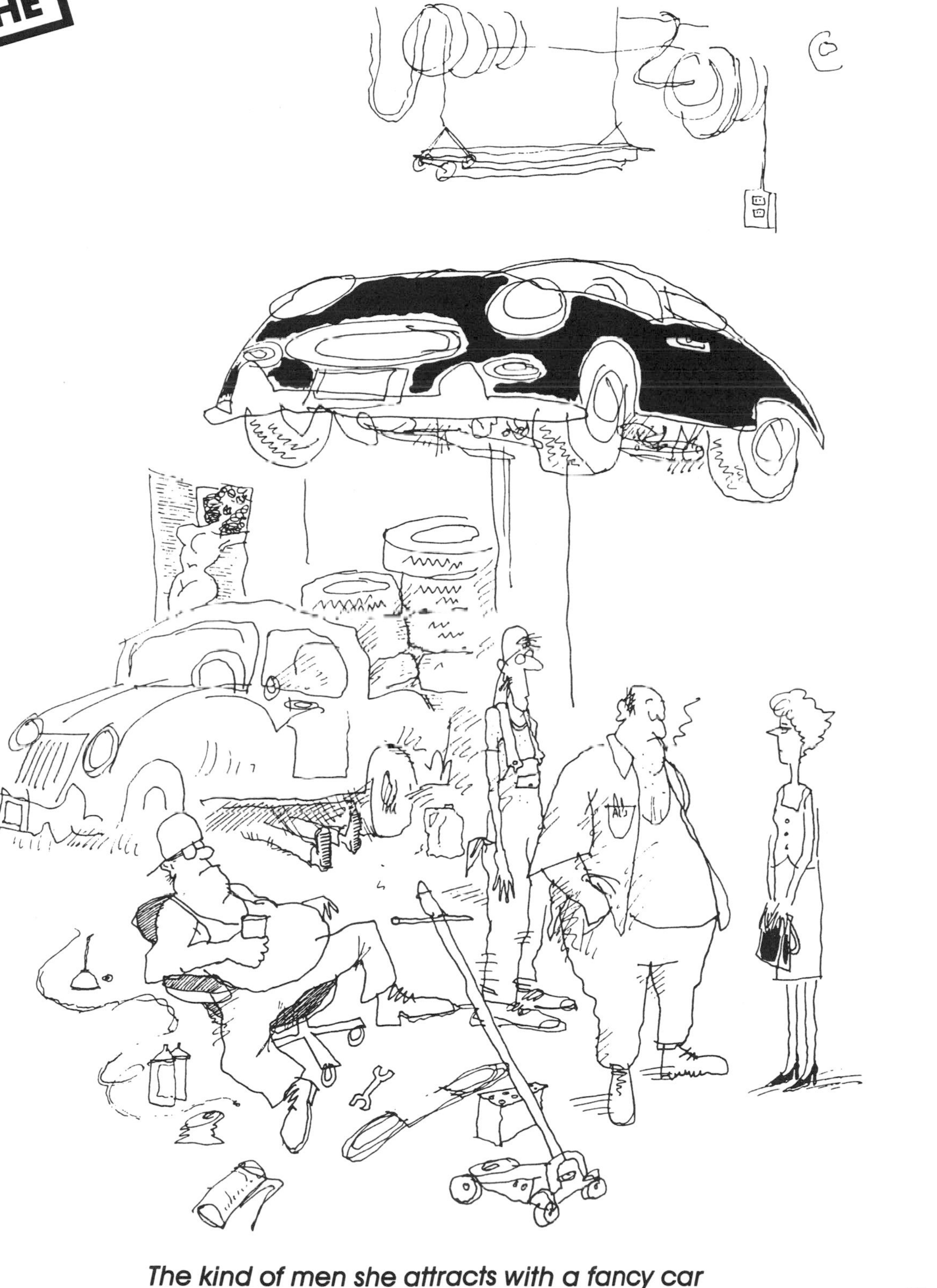

The kind of men she attracts with a fancy car

RULES OF THE ROAD TRIP

SHE

1) She will navigate, for good or ill.
2) She will suggest filling up when the tank is down to half.
3) She will look to the map as if it is a holy text.
4) If someone cuts them off she takes it in stride.
5) Once every forty minutes she will endure peeing in strange gas station rest rooms of dubious hygiene.

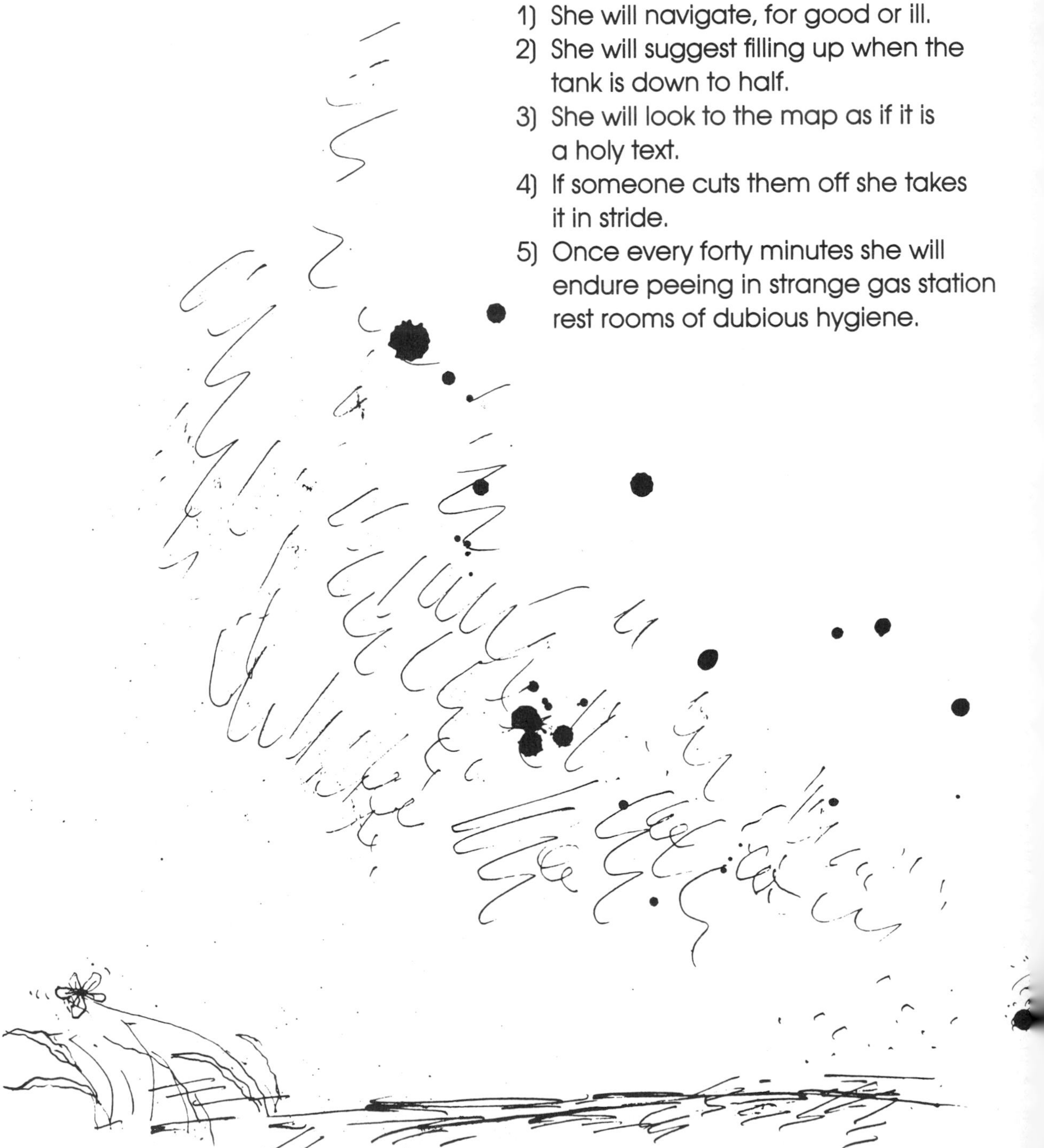

HE

1) He will drive, for good or ill.
2) He will drive on vapors.
3) He will not ask for directions, ever.
4) If someone cuts them off he takes it personally, assumes the persona of Road Warrior, and guns to avenge his honor and manhood.
5) Twice a day he will evacuate his bladder outside, in the open air, and enjoy it enormously.

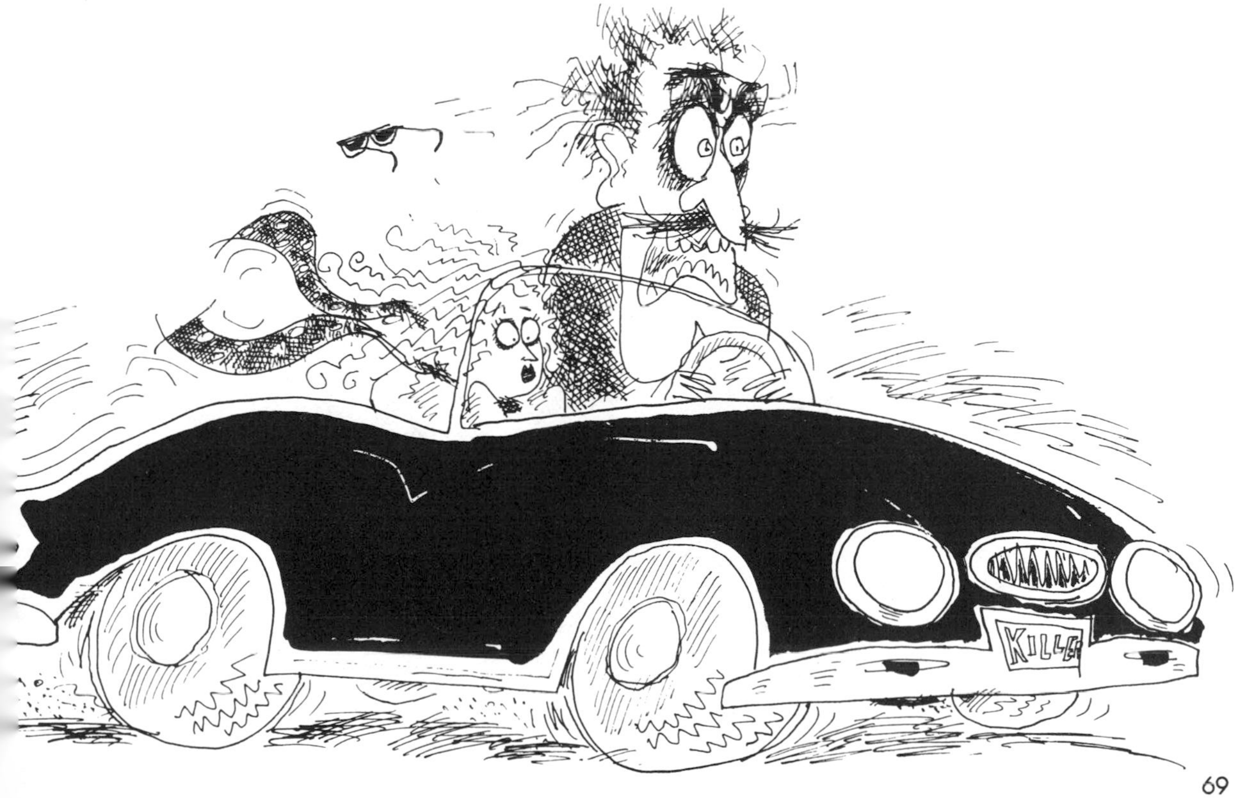
KILLER

PENIS ENVY

HE

"One cannot very well doubt the importance of envy for the penis. . . . As regards little girls, we can say of them that they feel greatly at a disadvantage owing to their lack of a big, visible penis, and that they envy boys for possessing one and that, in the main for this reason, they develop a wish to be a man—a wish that reemerges later on, in any neurosis that may arise if they meet with a mishap in playing the feminine part. . . . The girl's recognition of the fact of her being without a penis does not by any means imply that she submits to the fact easily. On the contrary, she continues to hold on for a long time to the wish to get something like it herself. . . ."

—Sigmund Freud

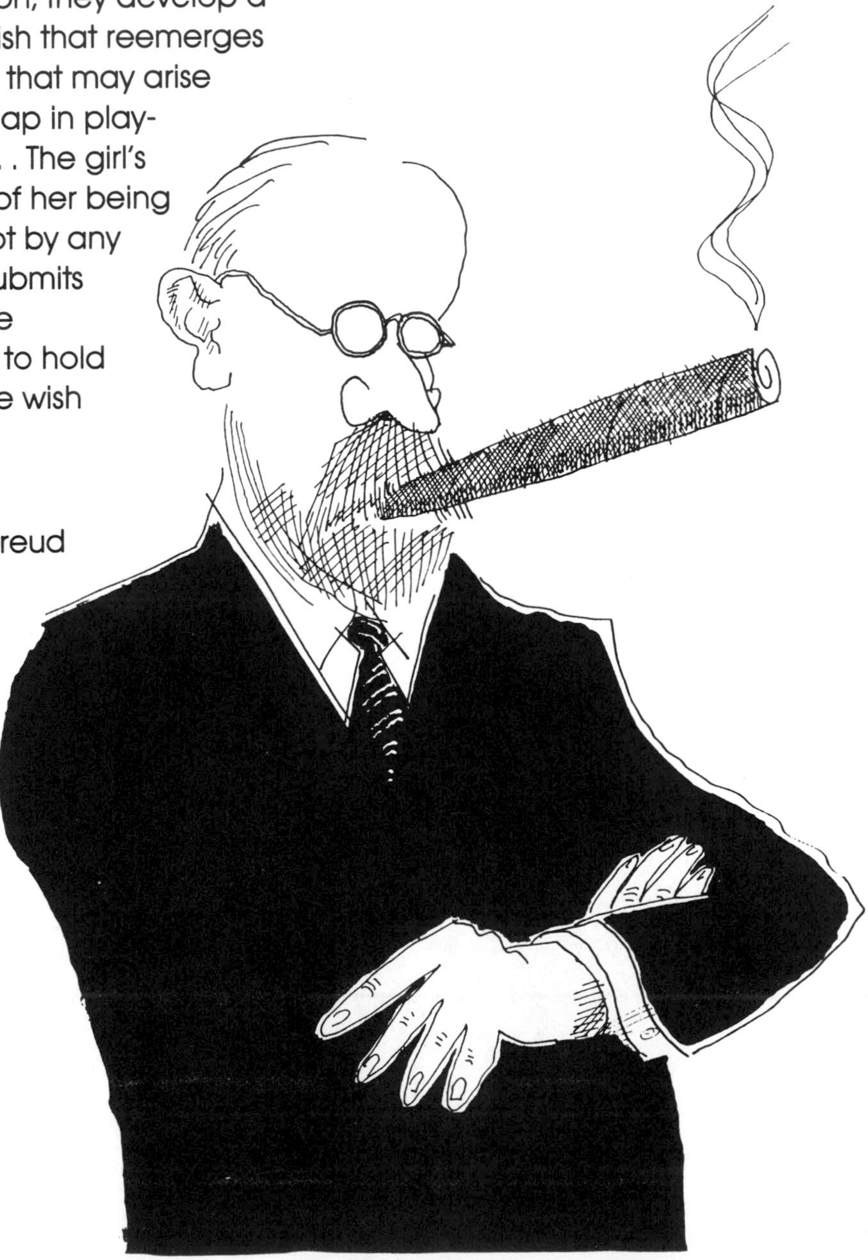

"I've already got enough flopping around on my body without one of those."

"Could I just get a raise in my salary instead?"

"Oh, please."

SET THEORY

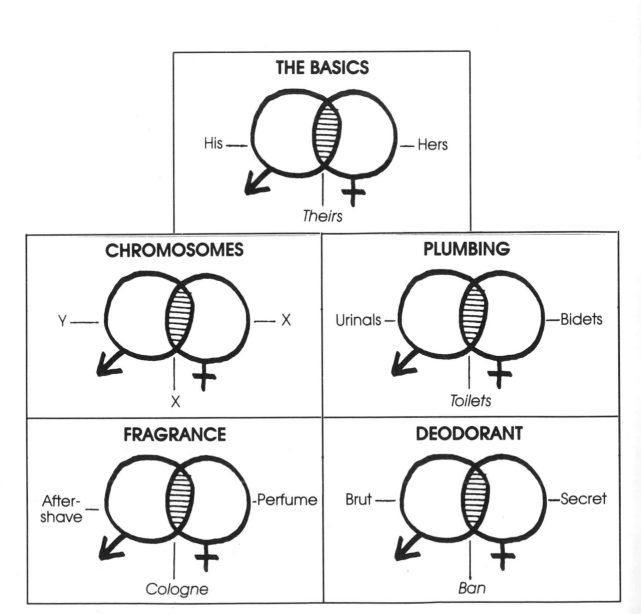

THE BASICS

His —— —— Hers

Theirs

CHROMOSOMES

Y —— —— X

X

PLUMBING

Urinals — —Bidets

Toilets

FRAGRANCE

After-shave — -Perfume

Cologne

DEODORANT

Brut — —Secret

Ban

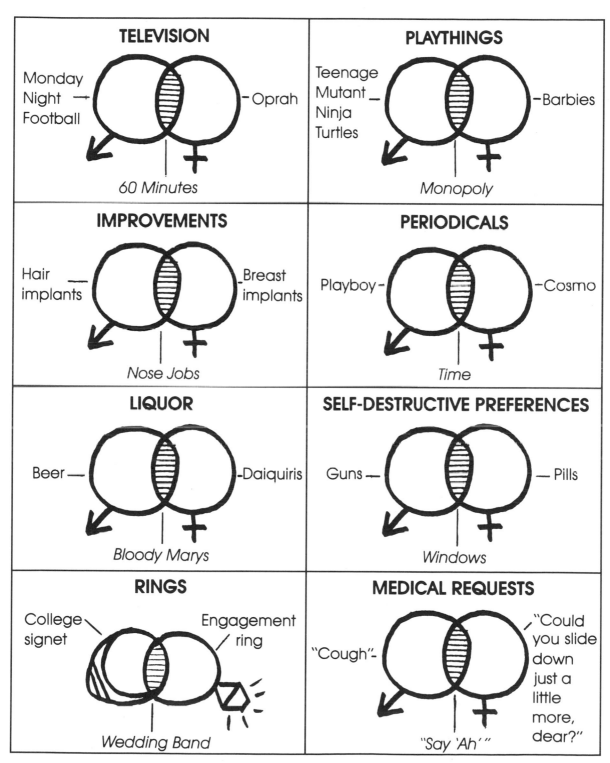

TELEVISION

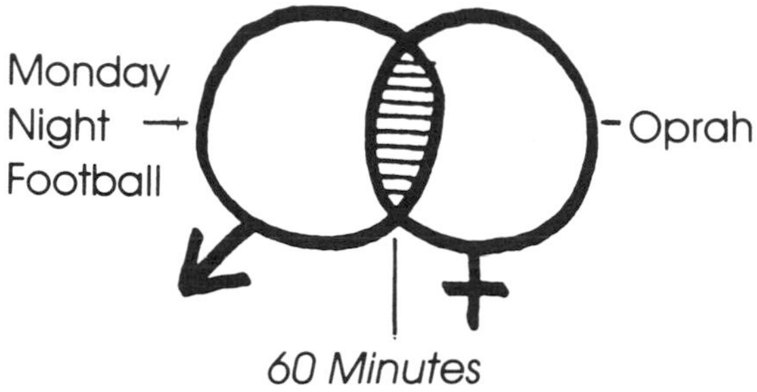
Monday Night Football
Oprah
60 Minutes

PLAYTHINGS

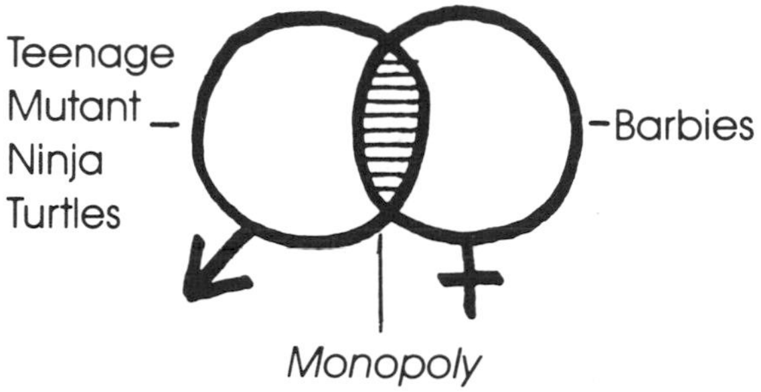
Teenage Mutant Ninja Turtles
Barbies
Monopoly

IMPROVEMENTS

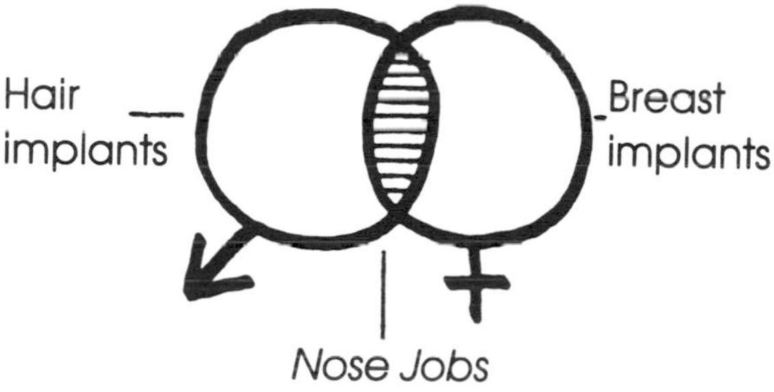
Hair implants
Breast implants
Nose Jobs

PERIODICALS

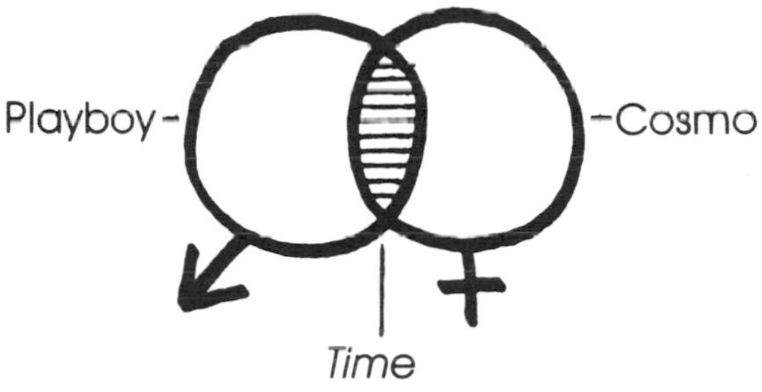
Playboy
Cosmo
Time

LIQUOR

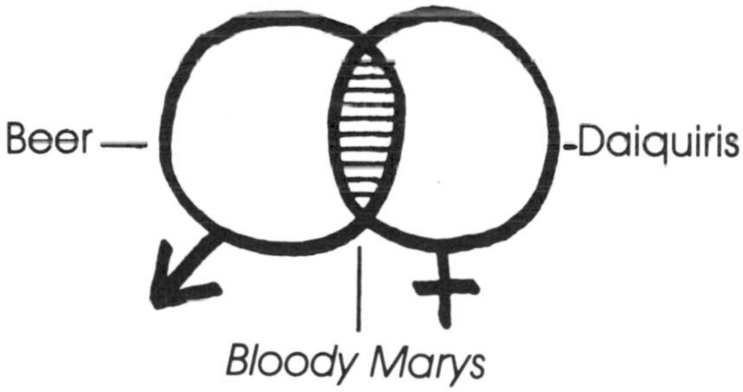
Beer
Daiquiris
Bloody Marys

SELF-DESTRUCTIVE PREFERENCES

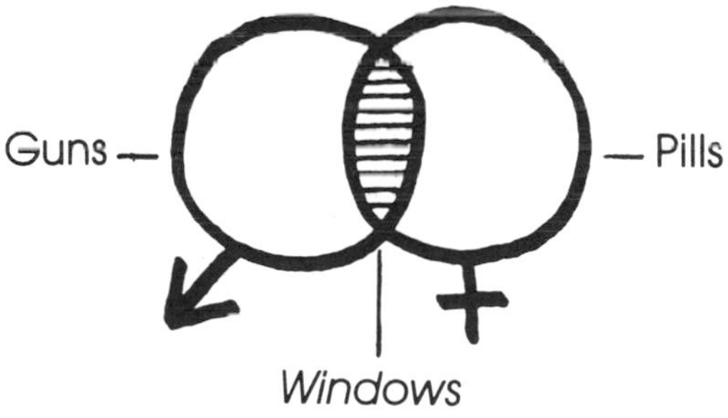
Guns
Pills
Windows

RINGS

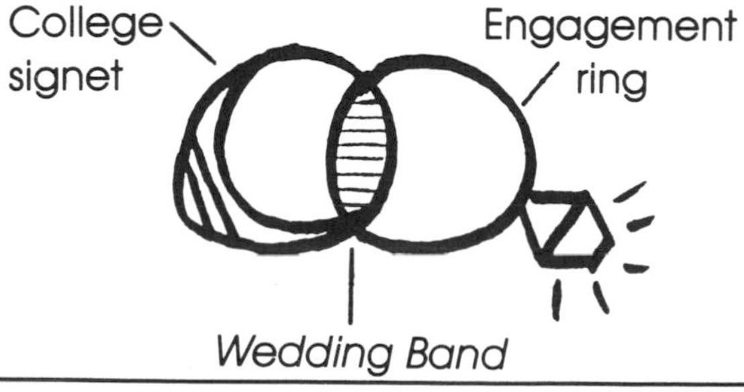
College signet
Engagement ring
Wedding Band

MEDICAL REQUESTS

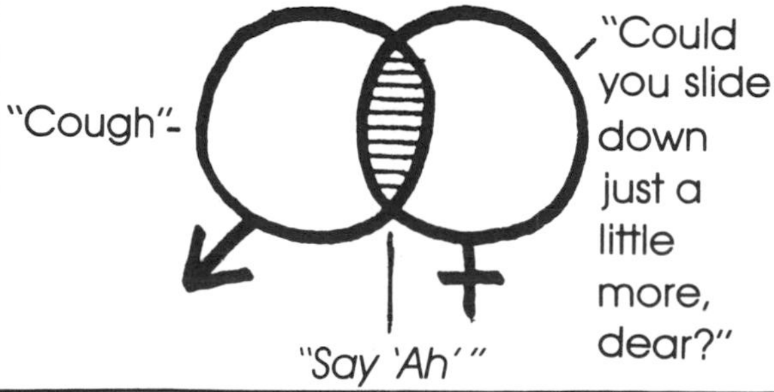
"Cough"
"Could you slide down just a little more, dear?"
"Say 'Ah'"

SITTING PRETTY

HE

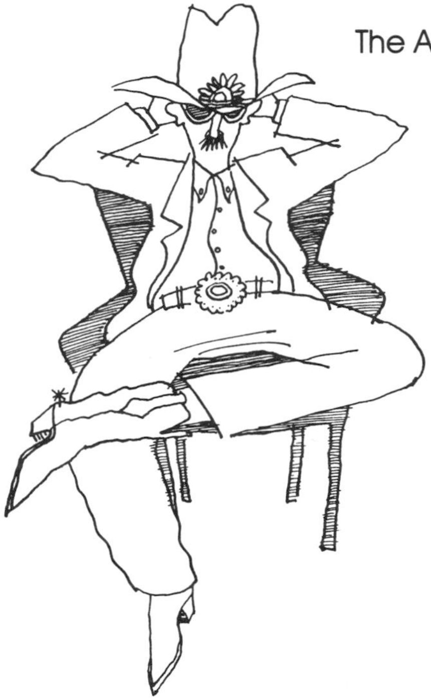

The American Cross

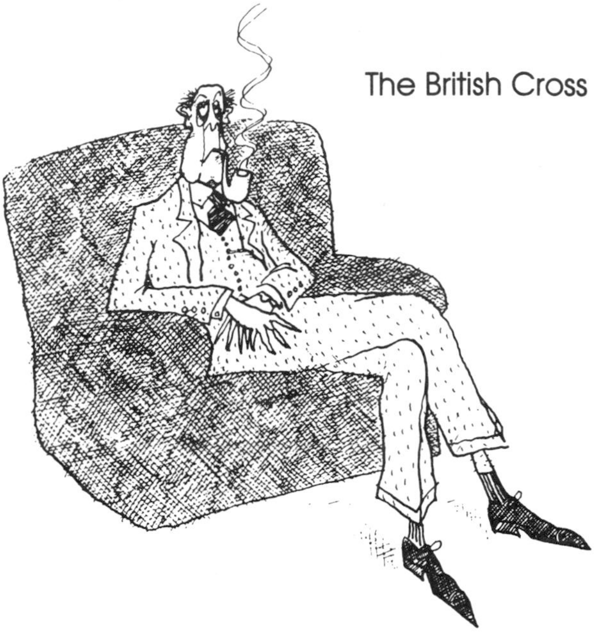

The British Cross

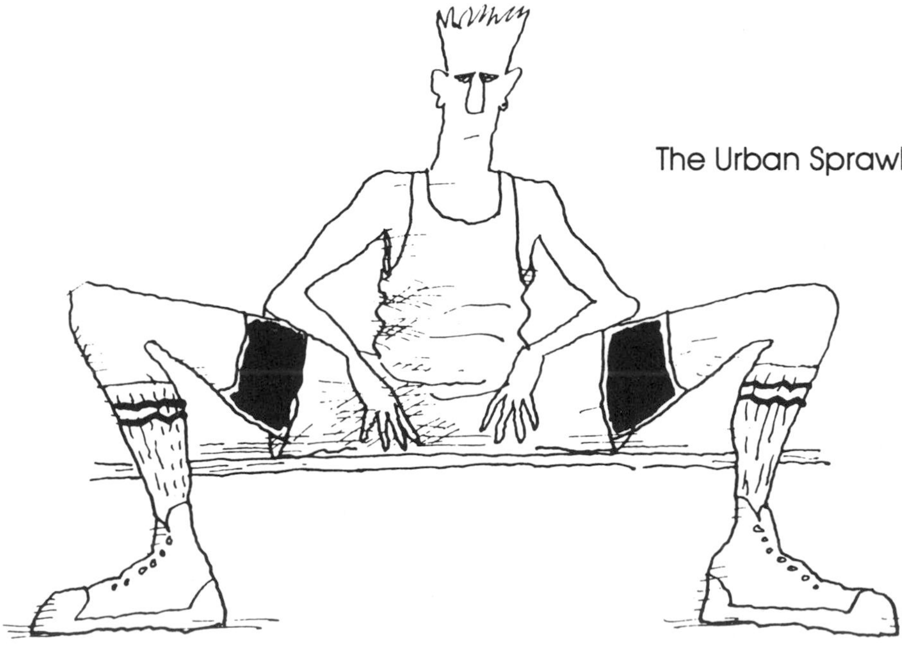

The Urban Sprawl

SHE

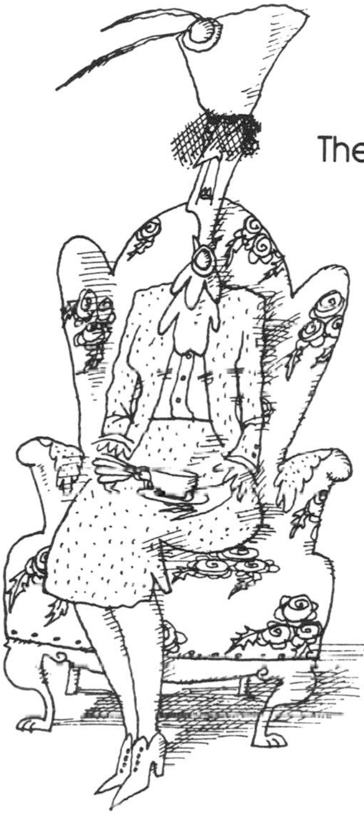

The Lady

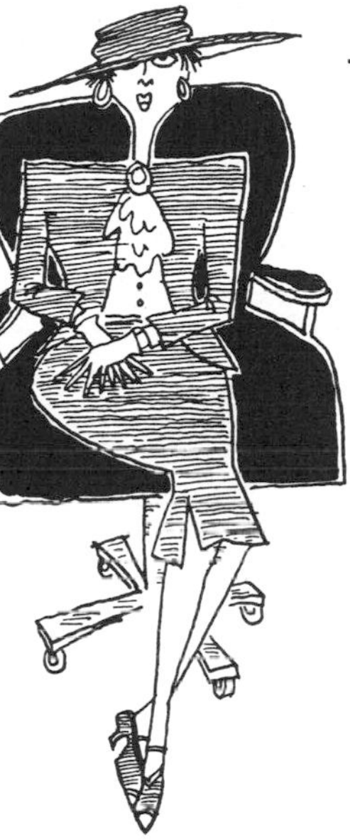

The Little Lady

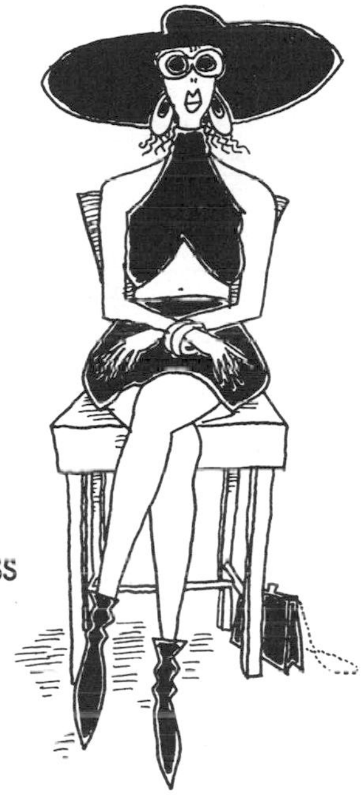

The Basic Cross

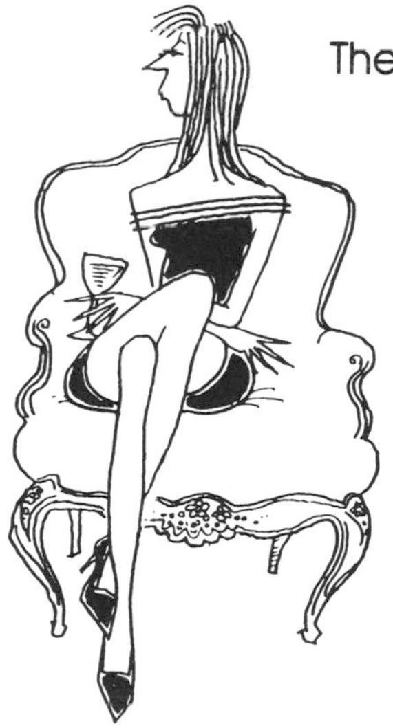

The Serpentine Cross

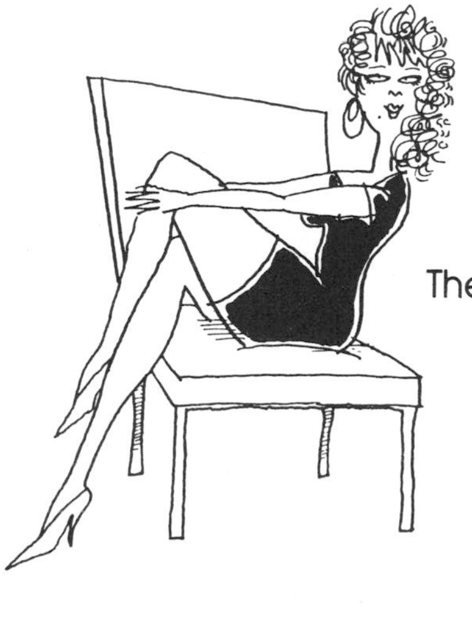

The Mistress Clutch

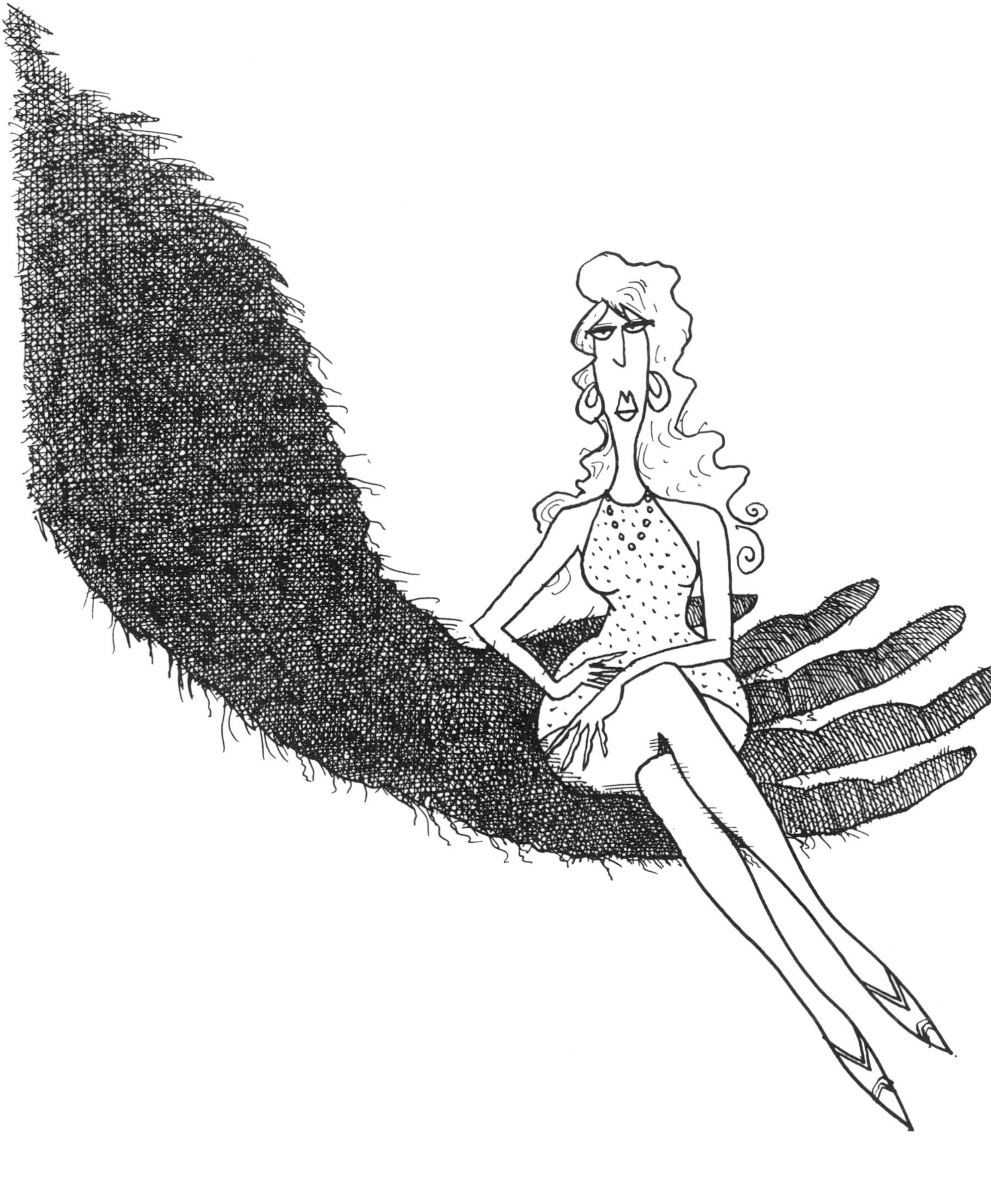

— CHAPTER V —

COMMUNICATION

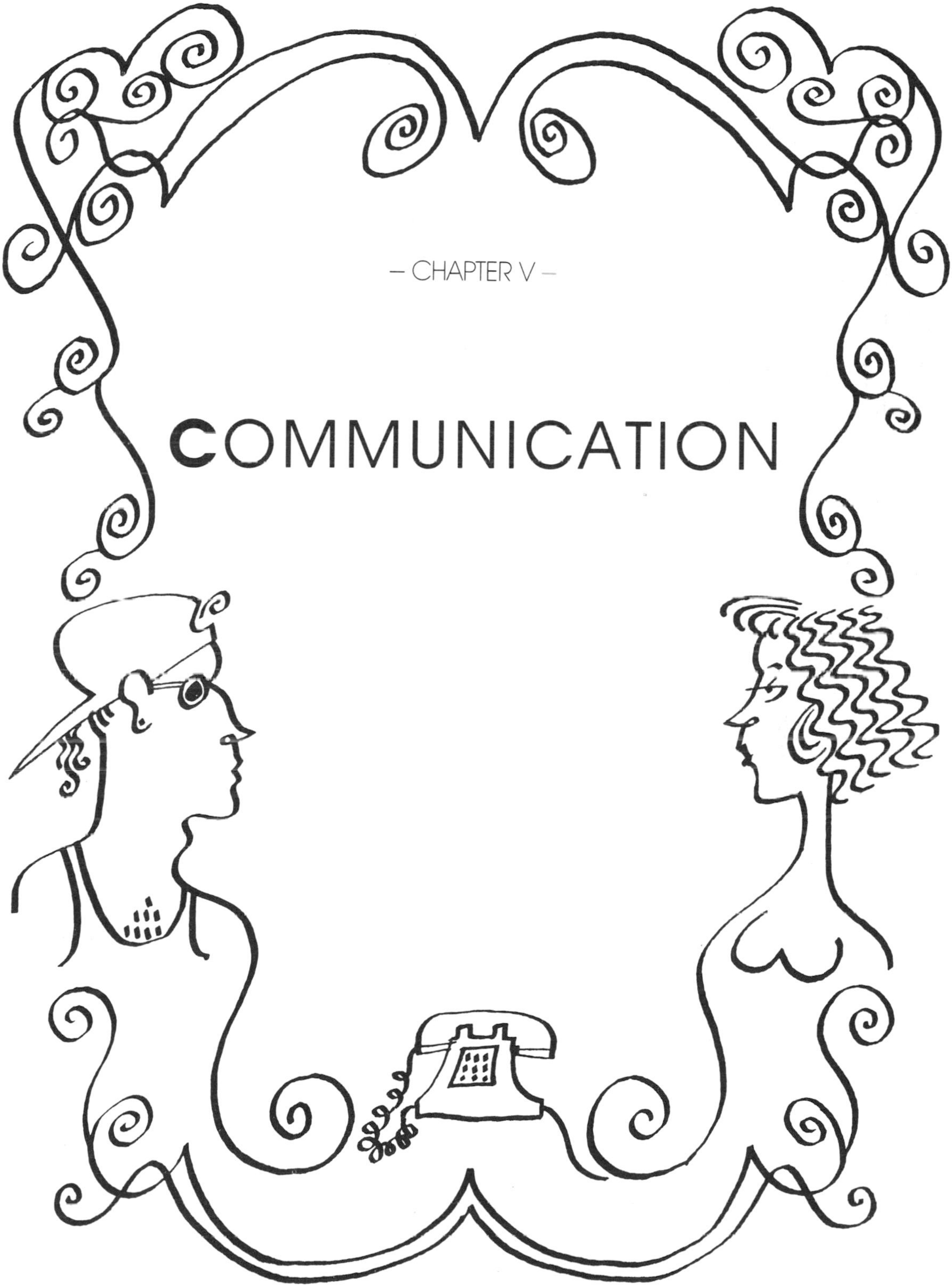

CONVERSATION TABULATION

HE

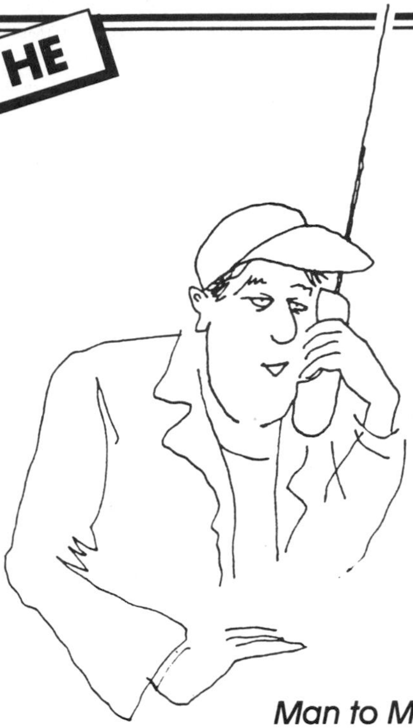

Man to Man

Greeting	5 seconds
Joke	30 seconds
Analysis of current events (i.e., the market)	30 seconds
Talk about sports and/or car	1 minute
Remarks on women*	20 seconds
Work update	30 seconds
Salutations	10 seconds
Total	3 minutes, 5 seconds

*Optional—Subtract from car time but not to take away from sports time

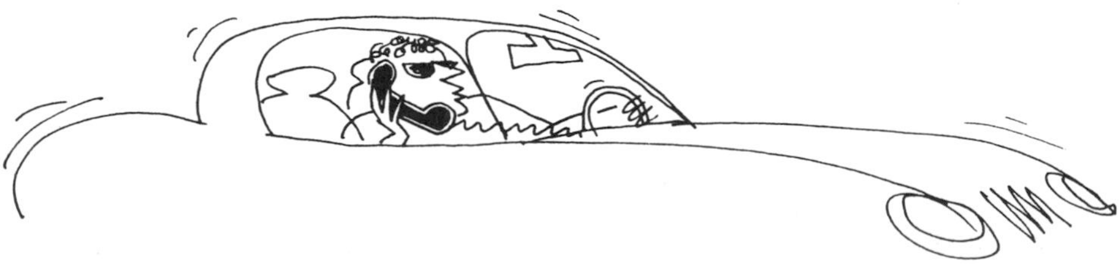

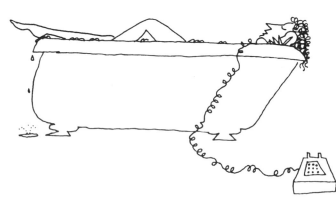

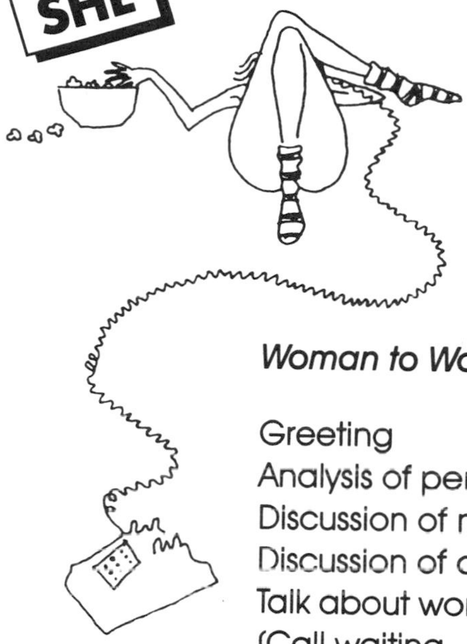

SHE

Woman to Woman

Greeting	10 seconds
Analysis of personal state of mind	12 minutes
Discussion of mate or lack thereof	27 minutes
Discussion of child or lack thereof	20 minutes
Talk about work	12 minutes
(Call waiting—it's your mother)	30 seconds
Gossip about people we like	15 minutes
Gossip about people we don't like	35 minutes
Analysis of current events	13 minutes
Shopping news (i.e., the market)	4 minutes
More analysis of personal state of mind	4 minutes
(Call waiting—your mother again, annoyed)	45 seconds
Winding down	3 minutes
Great anecdote that can't wait	7 minutes
Salutations	10 seconds
Total	2 hours, 33 minutes, 35 seconds

"I'LL CALL YOU" (a translation)

HE

It means:

"Don't call me."

"I've really got to leave."

"I want to be alone."

"I'm not actually interested in pursuing this any further."

"I'm busy for the rest of my life."

"Please don't ask . . . anything."

"It was fun for me too, babe."

"Hell will freeze over before I'd ever try to reach you again."

"You slept with me too soon."

"You didn't sleep with me soon enough."

"Actually, I'm already involved."

"Where are my shoes?"

"Shhhhhhh."

"So long, farewell, *auf Weidersehen, adieu!*"

"I'm outta here."

"Maybe I'll call you."

It means:

"I'll call you."

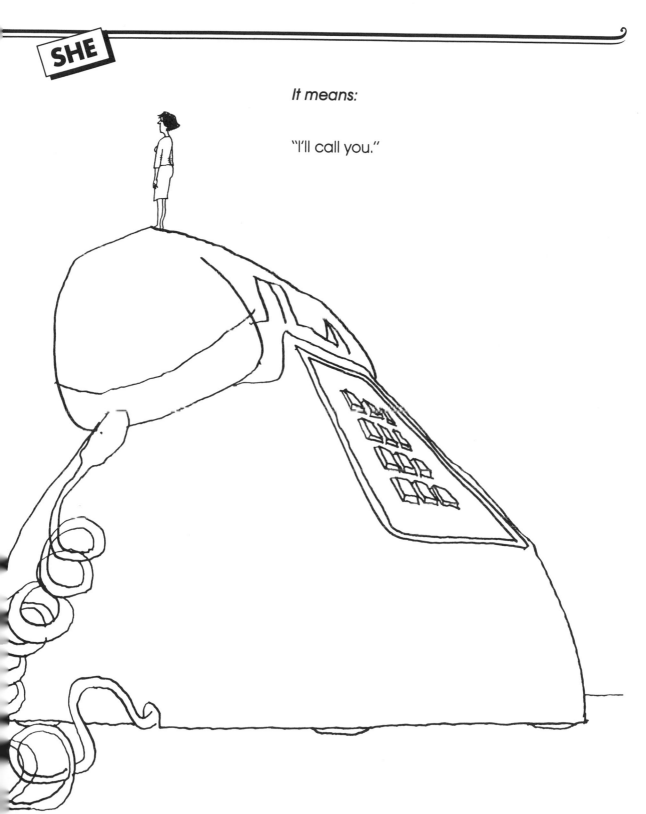

VITAL STATS

SHE

What she tells her friends about the man she's madly in love with:

Name, rank, and serial number
What he looks like
How he dresses
Word-for-word dialogue of every phone call
Play-by-play of every encounter (sexual or otherwise)
Vital stats and measurements (height, weight, hands, feet, inseam, genital, fat-to-lean muscle-mass ratio)
What he does for a living
Where he went to school
What kind of car he drives
Where he lives
How much money he's got
Who his best friend is
What kind of watch he wears
How/if he votes
How he lost his virginity
Ex-wives, girlfriends, and debris
Sexual style, technique, innuendo, and idiosyncrasies
If he's ever done jury duty
Astrological sign

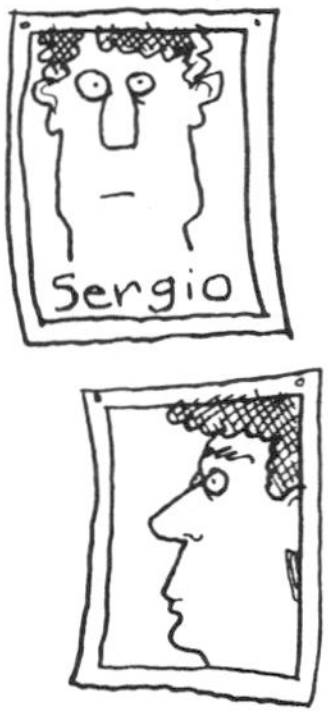
Sergio

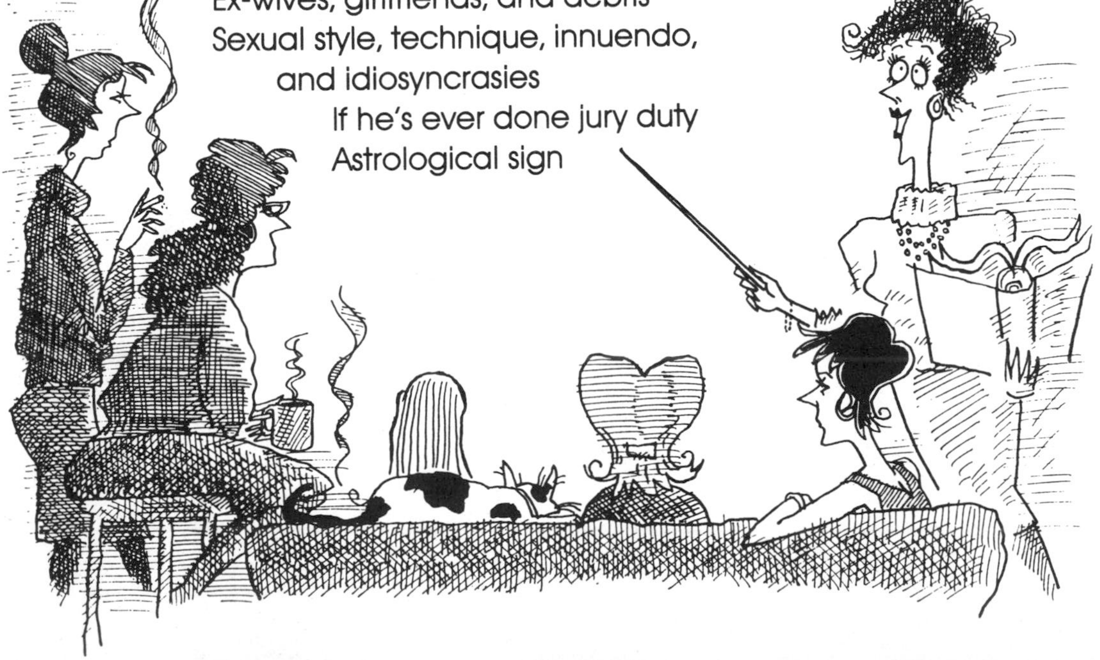

SAT scores
How he gets along with his parents
Mother's maiden name
Favorite foods
Favorite sport
Favorite movie
Favorite mind-altering substances
Favorite shirt
Habits, addictions, tics, and twitches
Brand of after-shave
Allergies
Every endearing thing he's
ever done, said, or
hinted at
Dental history and
cavity situation
Revealing personal details that
would kill him if he ever
had the faintest idea that
they were repeated

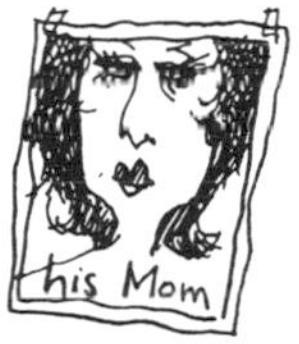
his Mom

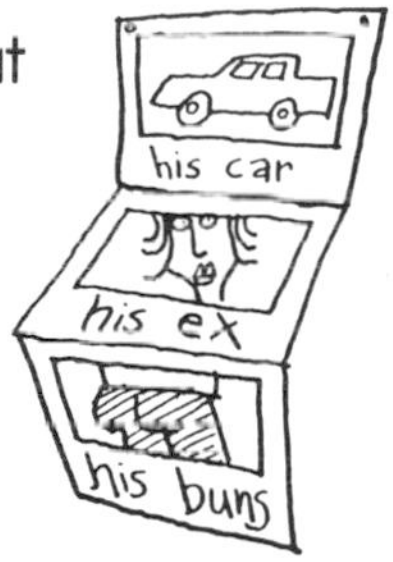
his car
his ex
his buns

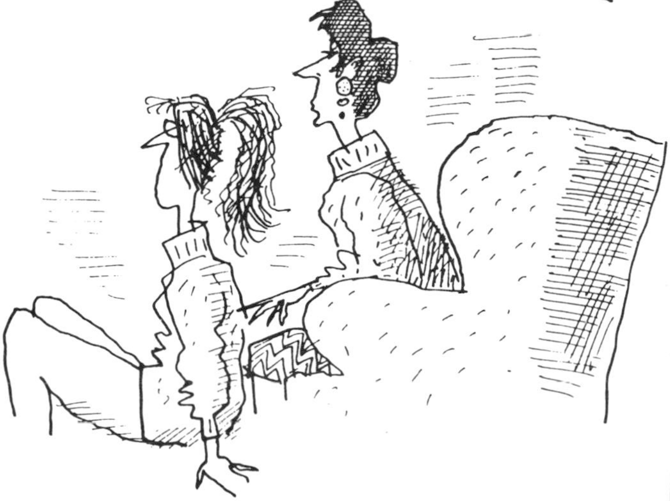

HE

What he tells his friends about the woman he's madly in love with:

She's nice

MISGUIDED GIFTS

HE

	What SHE Means	*How* HE Takes It
Cologne in decorative canister 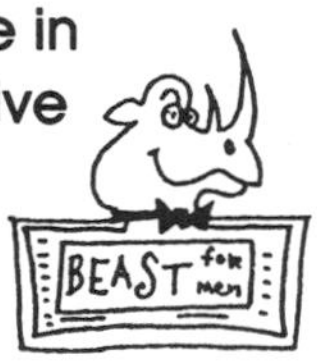 BEAST for men	"It's so sexy, so dangerous."	"Wear this and I'll smell like a gigolo."
Sweater 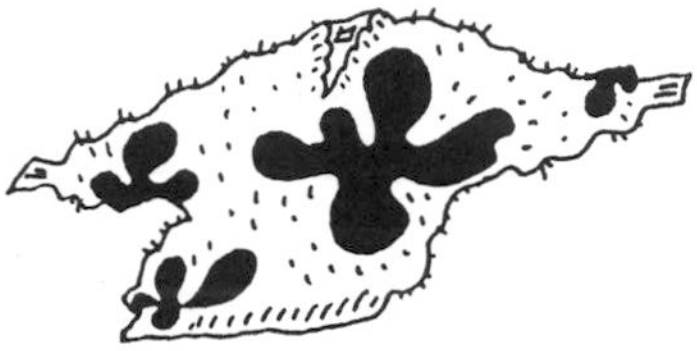	"It's Italian! It's designer! It's him!"	"Wear this and I'll look like a gigolo with fur."
Tie 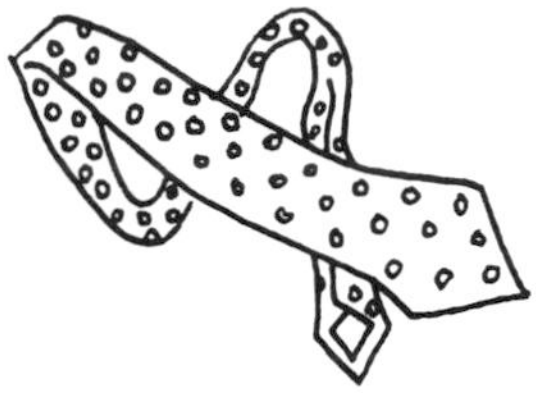	"It's Italian! It's designer! It's him!"	"She's strangling me."
Self-help books 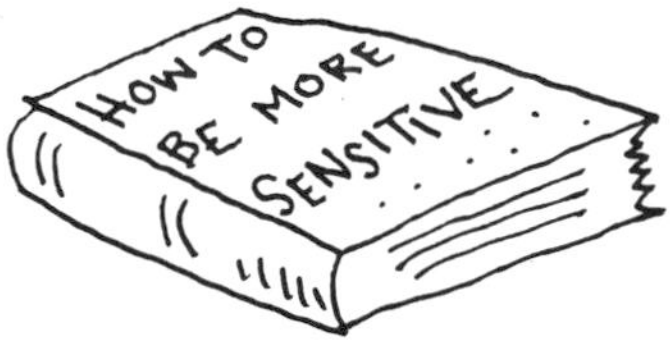 HOW TO BE MORE SENSITIVE	"This will help our relationship."	"She doesn't want me to go out with my friends anymore."
Sentimental jewelry 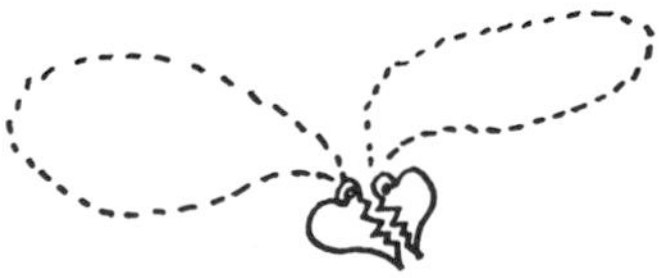	"He'll carry a little piece of me with him wherever he goes."	"I'm doomed."
Dustbuster 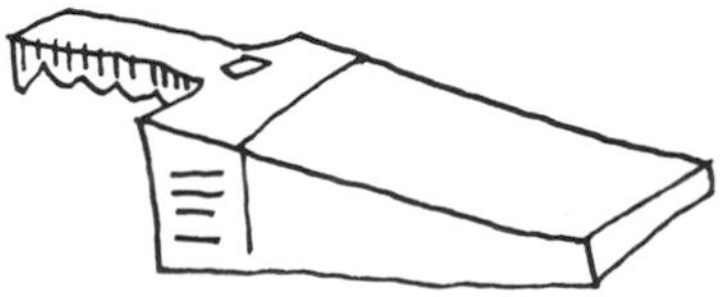	"Handy around the house."	"She wants to move in."

SHE	*What* HE Means	*How* SHE Takes It
Water Pik 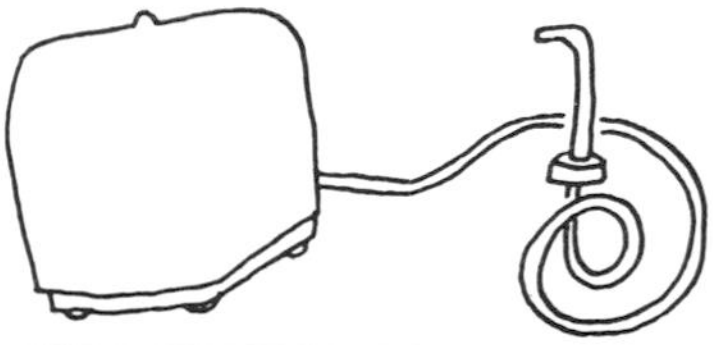	"It's something we'll both be able to use."	"He thinks I have coyote breath in the morning."
A rose 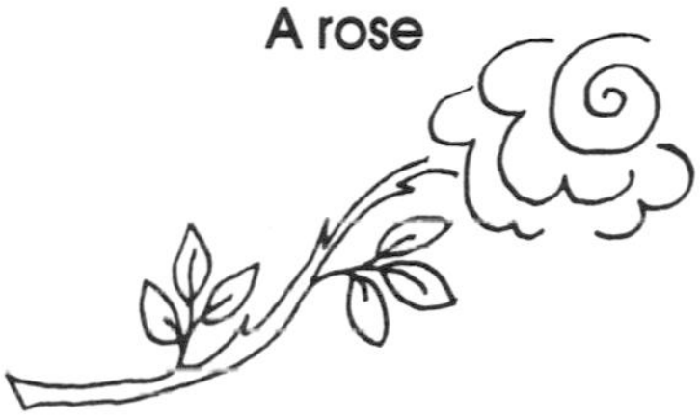	"A symbolic gesture signifying the singular purity of my emotion."	"He's too cheap to spring for a dozen."
Anything from the airport 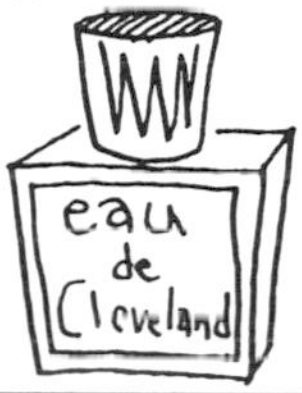 eau de Cleveland	"What a deal! Not only will she love this, it's duty-free."	"He doesn't care enough to take the time to shop."
Lingerie that doesn't fit 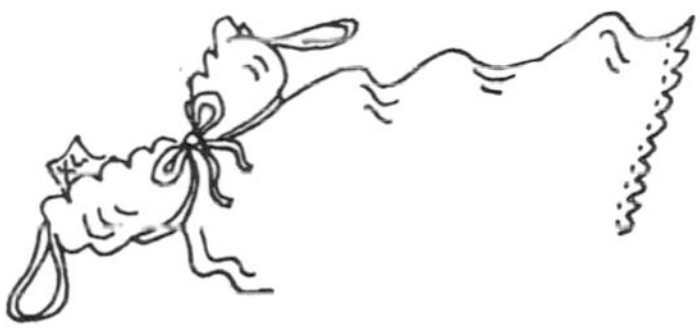	"Yowsa! We'll have fun with this."	"Not only does he think I'm a tramp, he thinks I'm a fat tramp."
Flat-tire repair kit 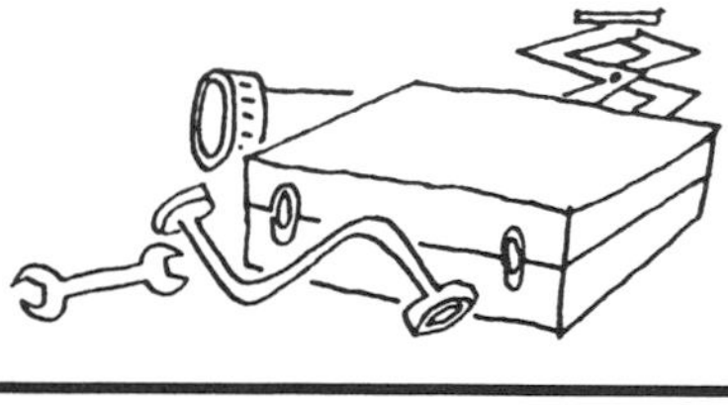	"This way she'll be okay if I'm not around."	"He's not planning on being around."
Dustbuster 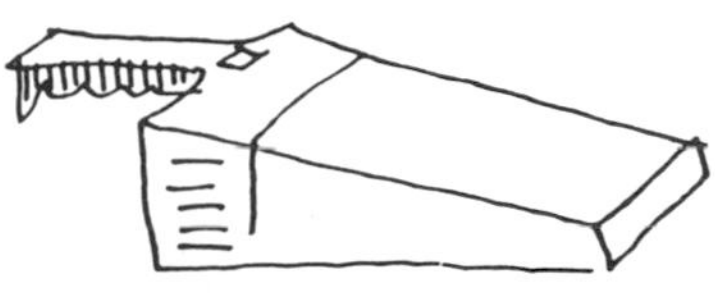	"Handy around the house."	"He wants to move out."

GREETINGS

SHE

Woman to Woman

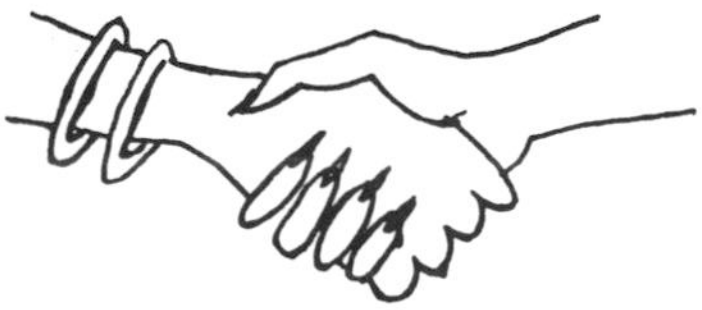

The Handshake

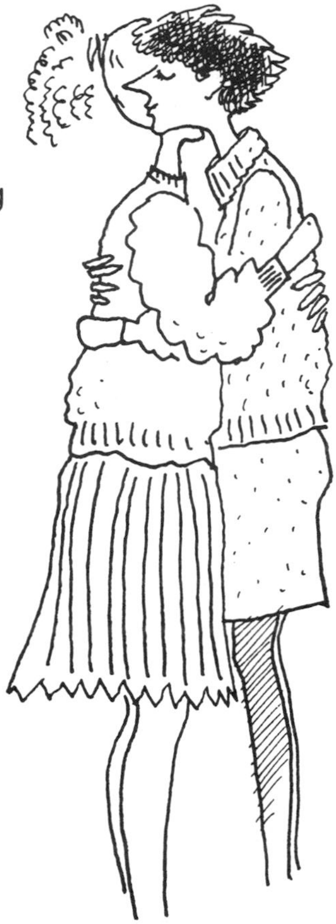

The Hug

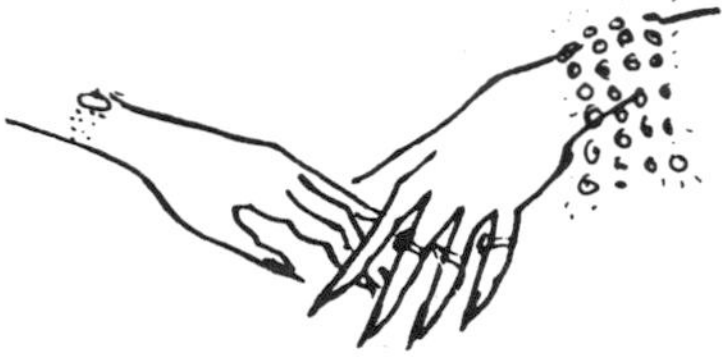

The Limp Fish
(misguided
notions of femininity)

The Kiss

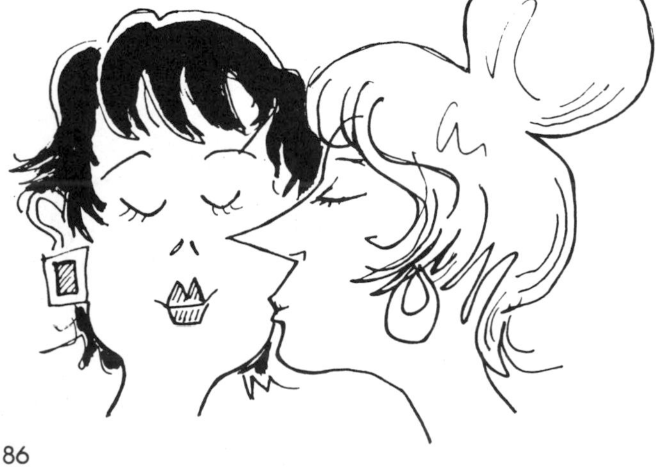

The Hollywood
Air Kiss

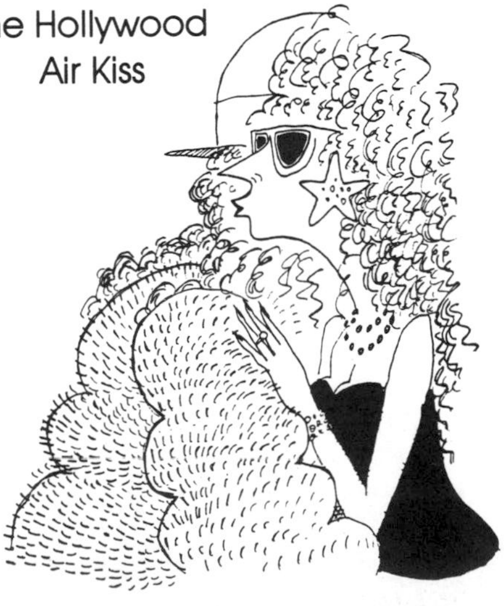

Man to Man

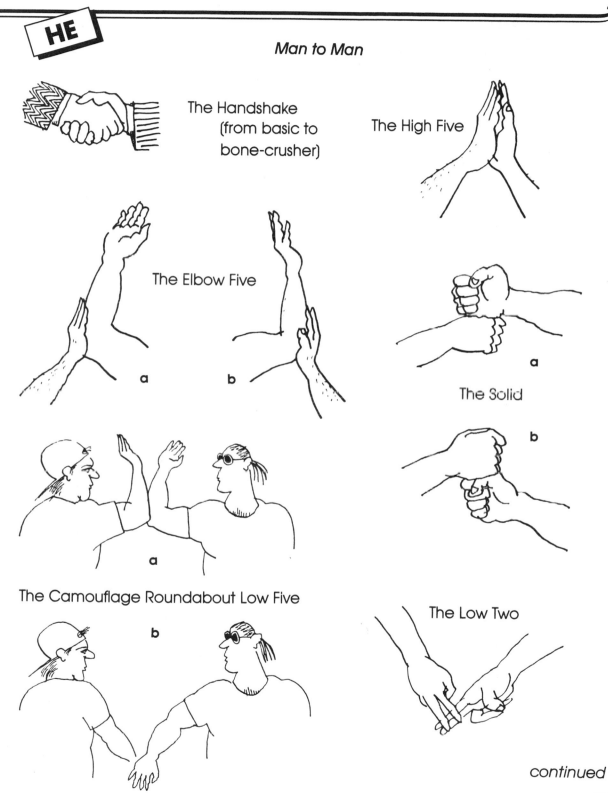

The Handshake
(from basic to
bone-crusher)

The High Five

The Elbow Five

a   b

a

The Solid

b

a

The Camouflage Roundabout Low Five

b

The Low Two

continued

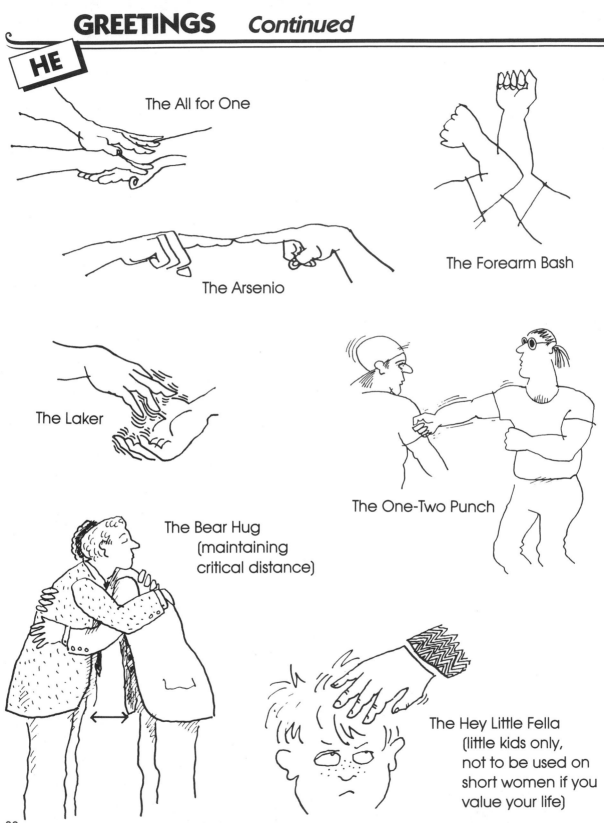

HE

The All for One

The Forearm Bash

The Arsenio

The Laker

The One-Two Punch

The Bear Hug
(maintaining
critical distance)

The Hey Little Fella
(little kids only,
not to be used on
short women if you
value your life)

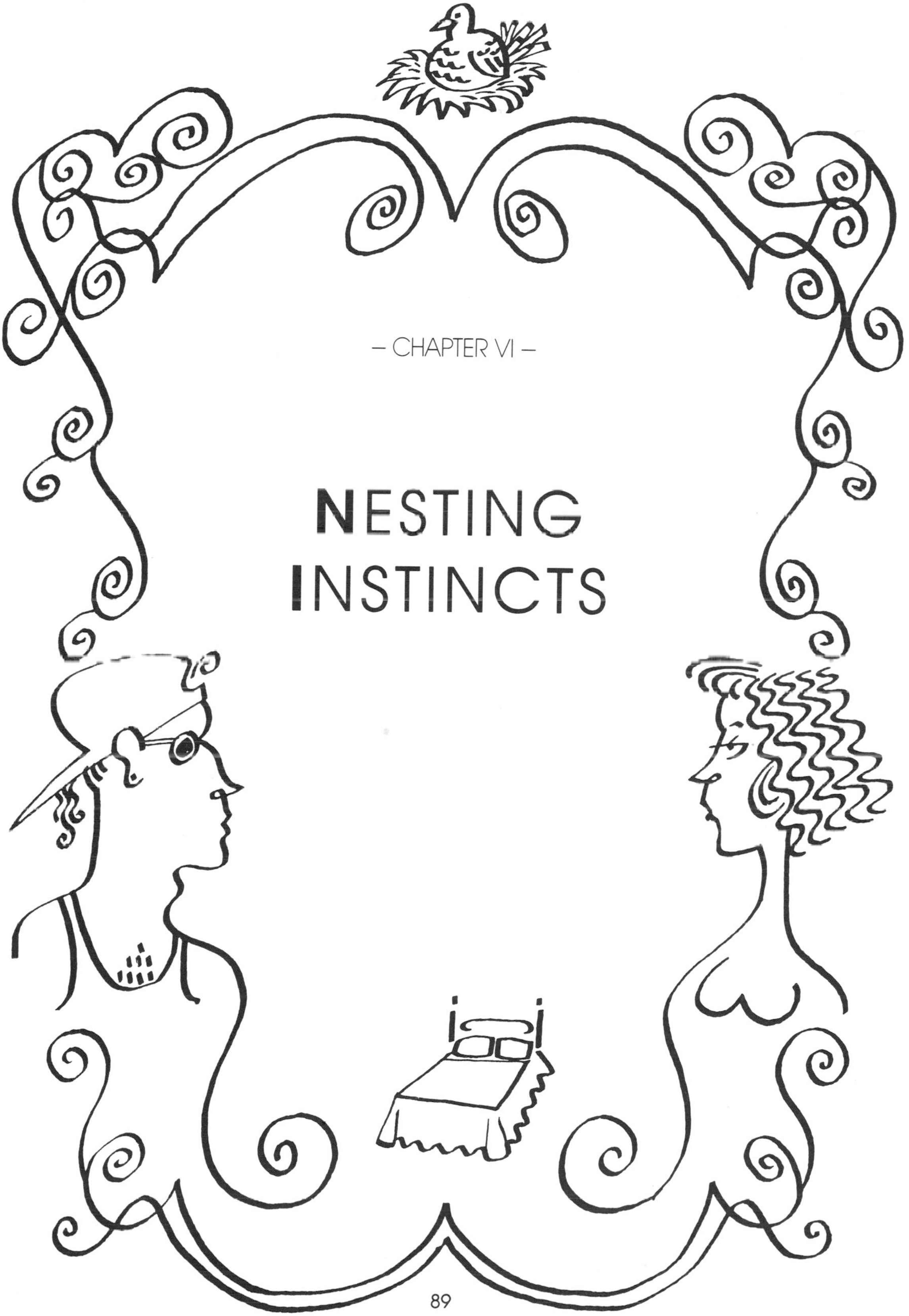

– CHAPTER VI –

NESTING INSTINCTS

INTERIOR DECORATION *Essential Elements*

HE

1) TV
2) Sound system
3) Bad carpeting

Bad Carpeting Color Palette

BACHELOR BEIGE
ALPO BROWN
GUACAMOLE
MICHELOB & MUSTARD
INDOOR/OUTDOOR ASTROTURF

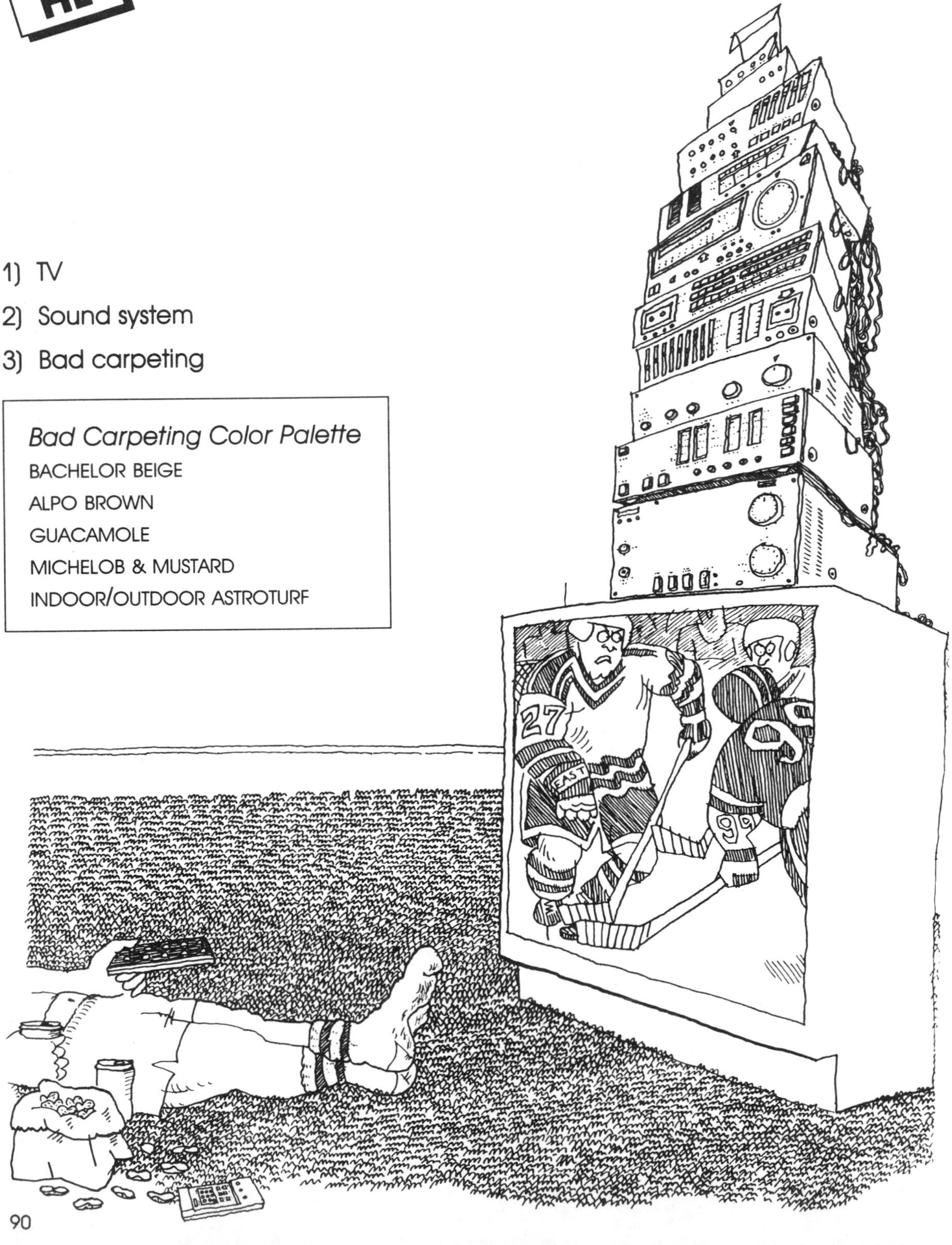
27
EAST
99

SHE

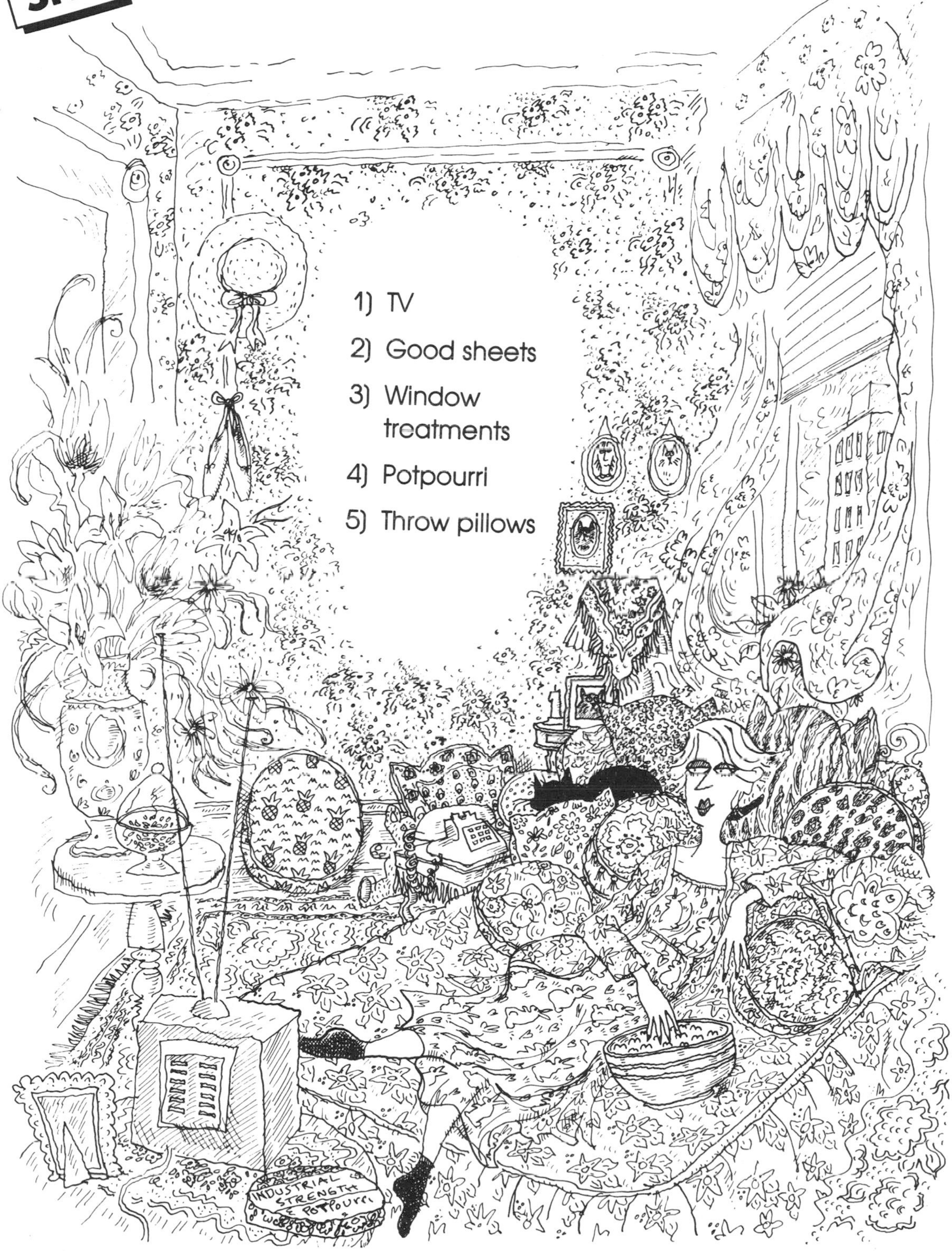
1) TV
2) Good sheets
3) Window treatments
4) Potpourri
5) Throw pillows
INDUSTRIAL STRENGTH POTPOURRI

LAUNDROLOGY

HE

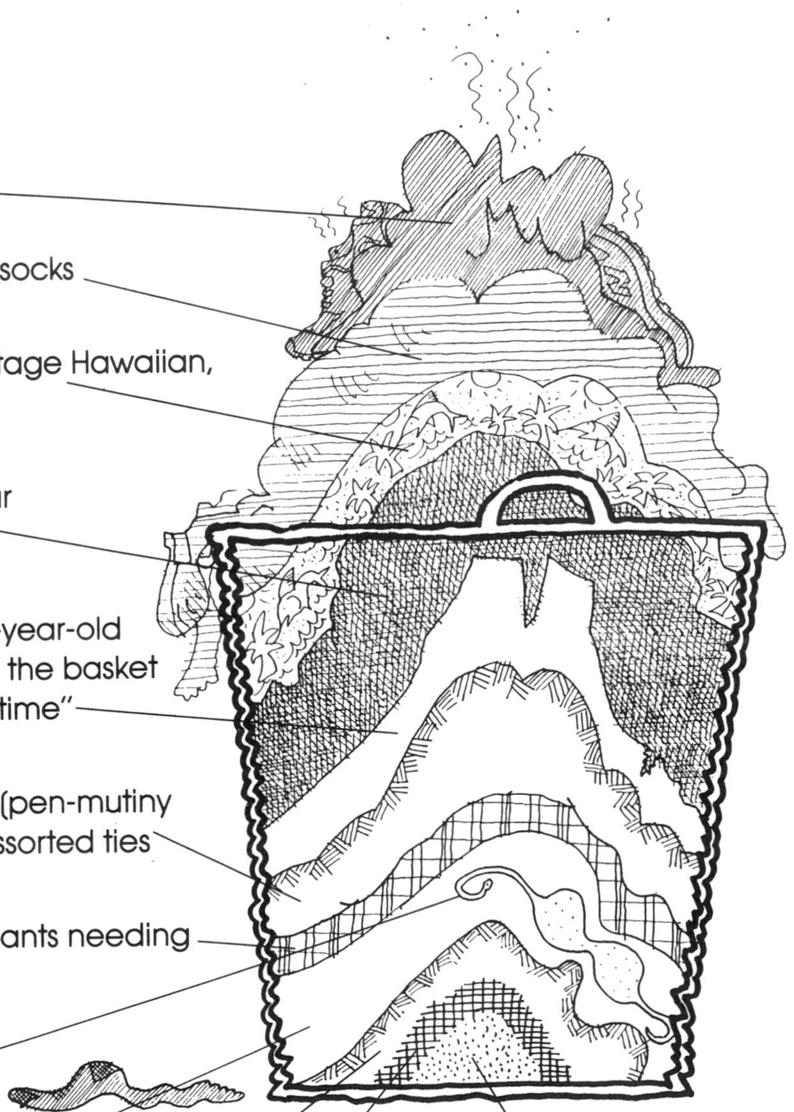

LAST THURSDAY
Softball stuff

1 WEEK
Assorted sweats, jocks, and socks

1½ WEEKS
Shirts (2 stripe, 2 plain, 1 vintage Hawaiian, and various T's)

3 WEEKS
20 days worth of underwear (time to buy new)

1 MONTH
Never-been-washed three-year-old jeans that go in and out of the basket to be worn "just one more time"

6 MONTHS
Dry cleaning: sports jacket (pen-mutiny victim), overcoat, chinos, assorted ties

2 YEARS
Shirt with missing buttons, pants needing new zipper

2¾ YEARS
Bra belonging to ????

3 Years
Bleeding purple towels requiring their own load

3 YEARS, 1 WEEK
Dingy purple-tinted underwear

PREHISTORY
$5.38 in change, single sock missing since 1978 (mate thrown away in 1983)

PRE-PREHISTORY
Compost

What Your Dirty Linen Says About You

SHE

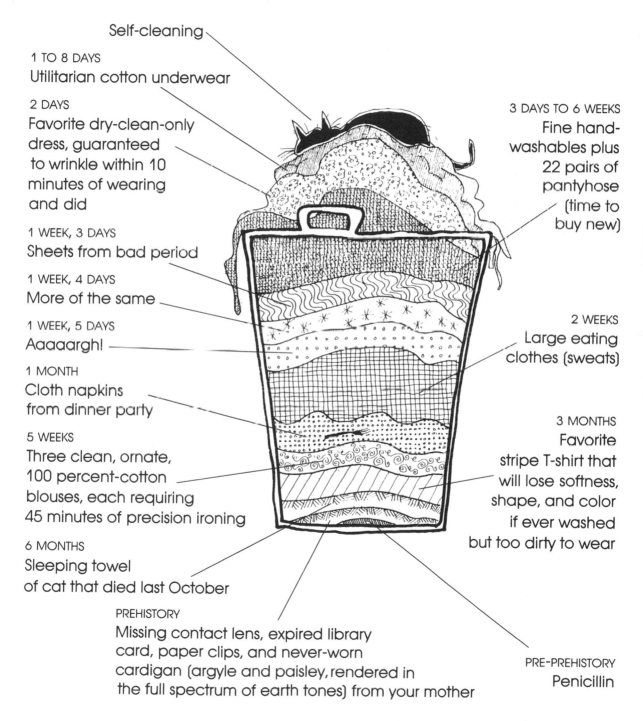

Self-cleaning
1 TO 8 DAYS
Utilitarian cotton underwear
2 DAYS
Favorite dry-clean-only dress, guaranteed to wrinkle within 10 minutes of wearing and did
1 WEEK, 3 DAYS
Sheets from bad period
1 WEEK, 4 DAYS
More of the same
1 WEEK, 5 DAYS
Aaaaargh!
1 MONTH
Cloth napkins from dinner party
5 WEEKS
Three clean, ornate, 100 percent-cotton blouses, each requiring 45 minutes of precision ironing
6 MONTHS
Sleeping towel of cat that died last October
PREHISTORY
Missing contact lens, expired library card, paper clips, and never-worn cardigan (argyle and paisley, rendered in the full spectrum of earth tones) from your mother
3 DAYS TO 6 WEEKS
Fine hand-washables plus 22 pairs of pantyhose (time to buy new)
2 WEEKS
Large eating clothes (sweats)
3 MONTHS
Favorite stripe T-shirt that will lose softness, shape, and color if ever washed but too dirty to wear
PRE-PREHISTORY
Penicillin

BATHROOM RATIOS

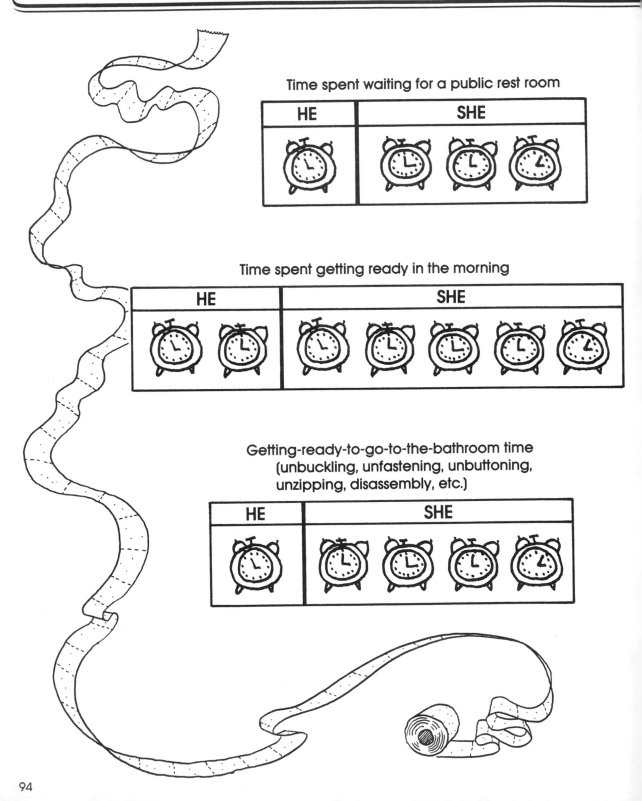

Time spent waiting for a public rest room

HE	SHE

Time spent getting ready in the morning

HE	SHE

Getting-ready-to-go-to-the-bathroom time
(unbuckling, unfastening, unbuttoning,
unzipping, disassembly, etc.)

HE	SHE

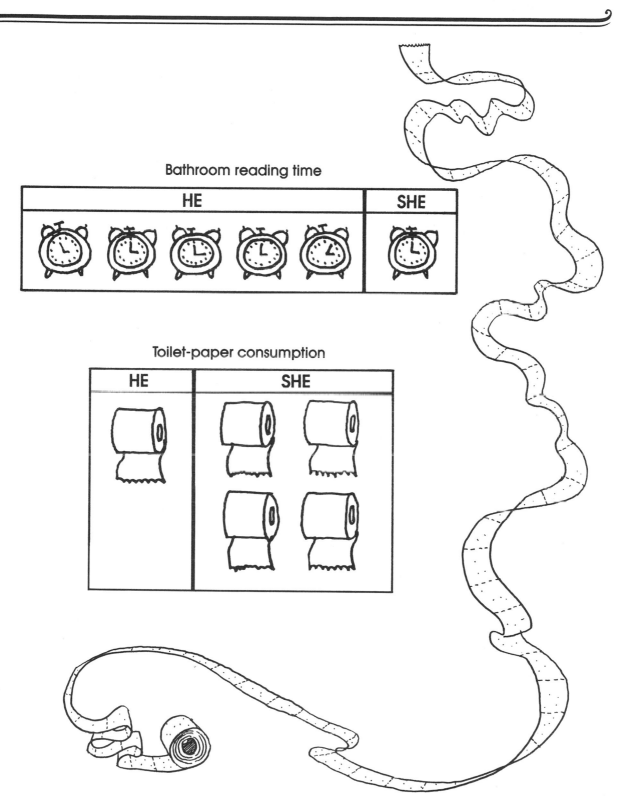

Bathroom reading time

HE	SHE

Toilet-paper consumption

HE	SHE

ROOM TEMPERATURE

HE

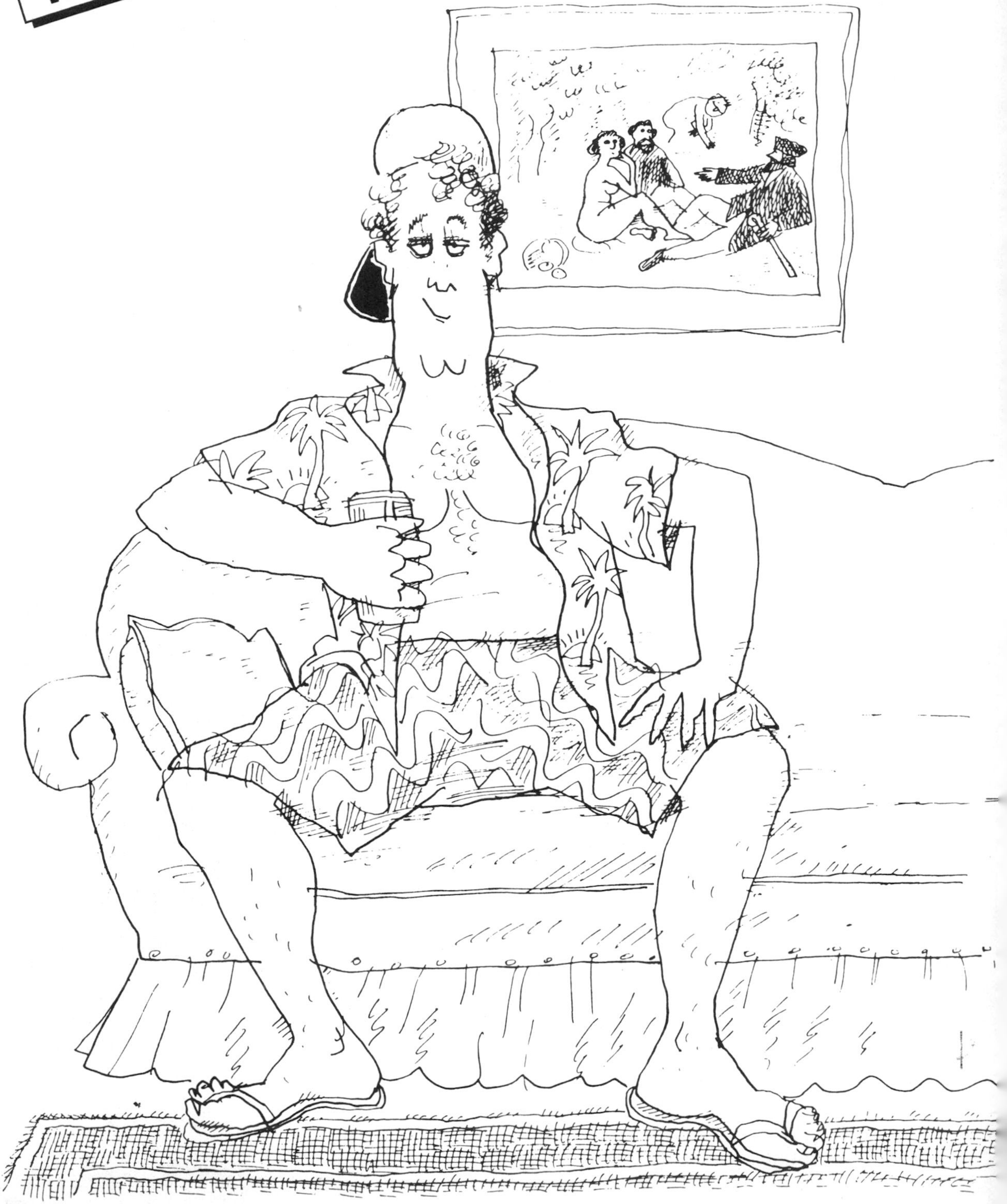

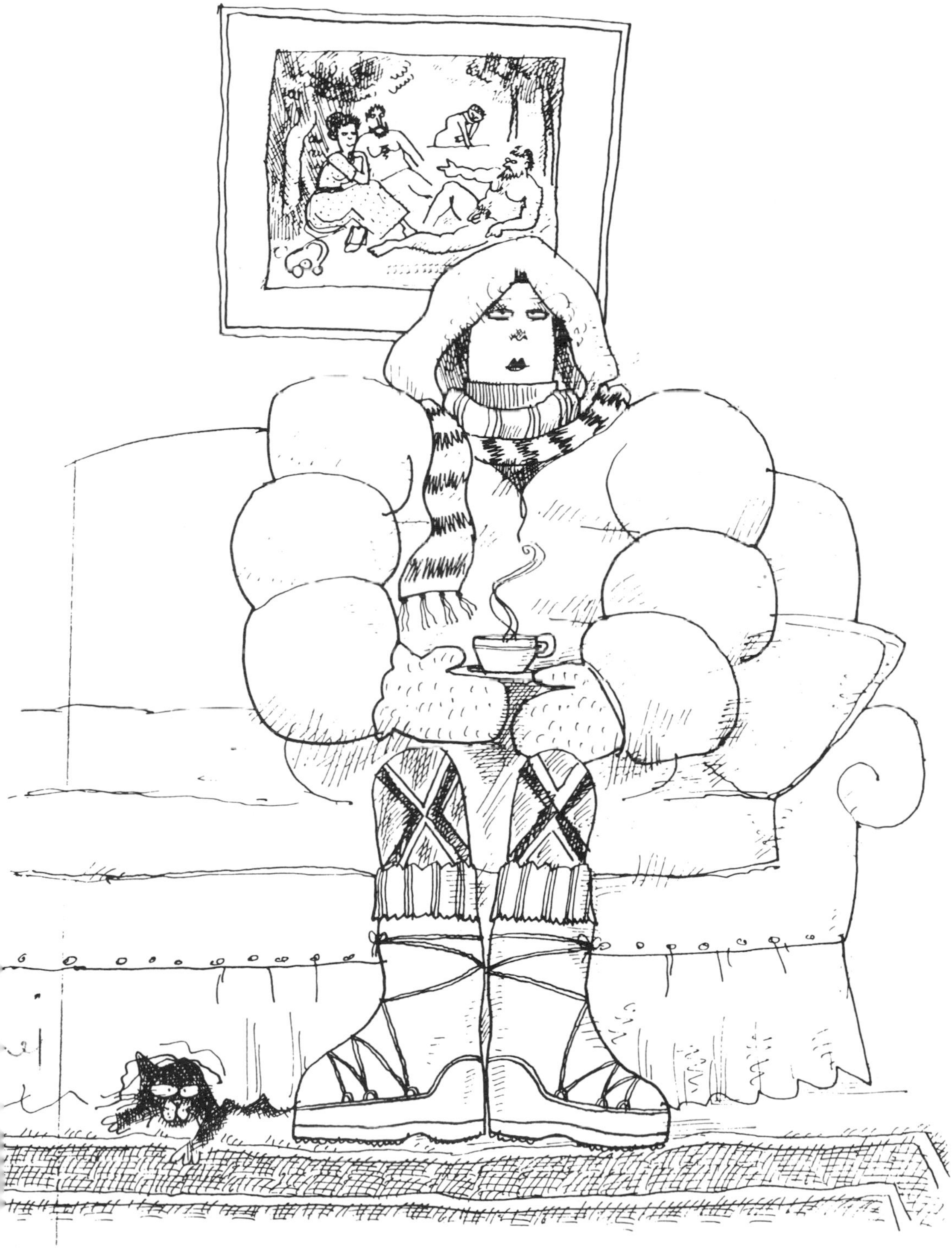

TELLTALE SIGNS

HE

How he figures she's been untrue:

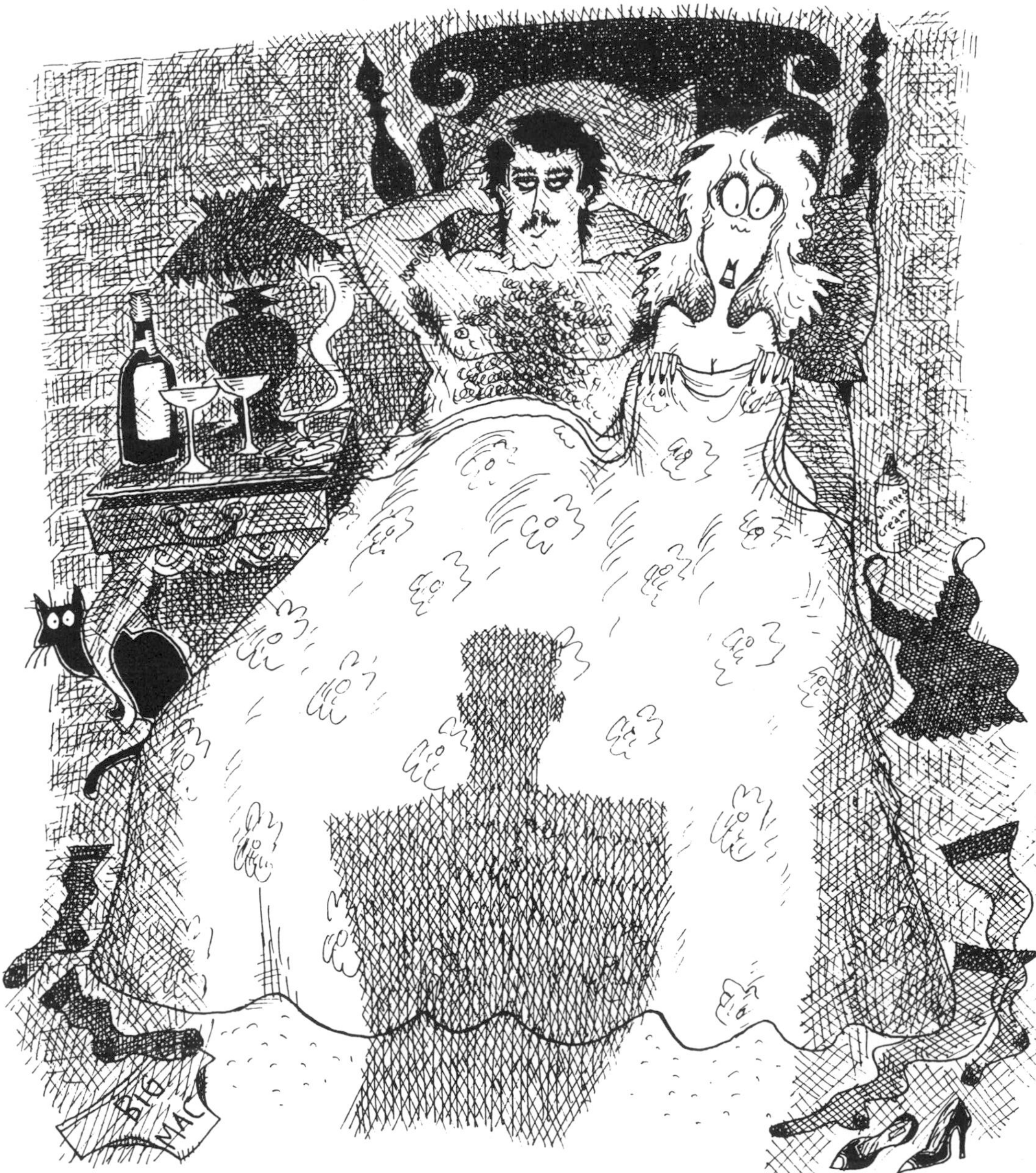
Whipped Cream
BIG MAC

There's a big hairy guy in her bed.

How she figures he's been untrue:

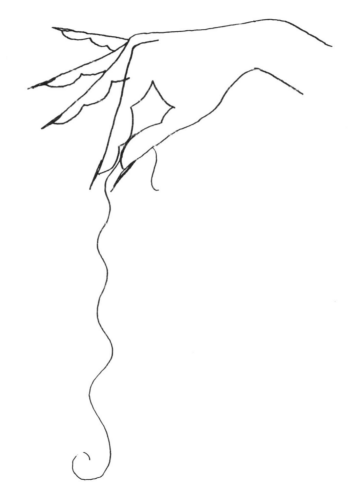

There's a hair there.

A WORLD WITHOUT MEN

SHE

1) A marked increase in the sales of sweat clothes.
2) No more birth control.
3) No more girth control.
4) Grooming gets easier.
5) Everybody in the entire world would get her period on the same day.

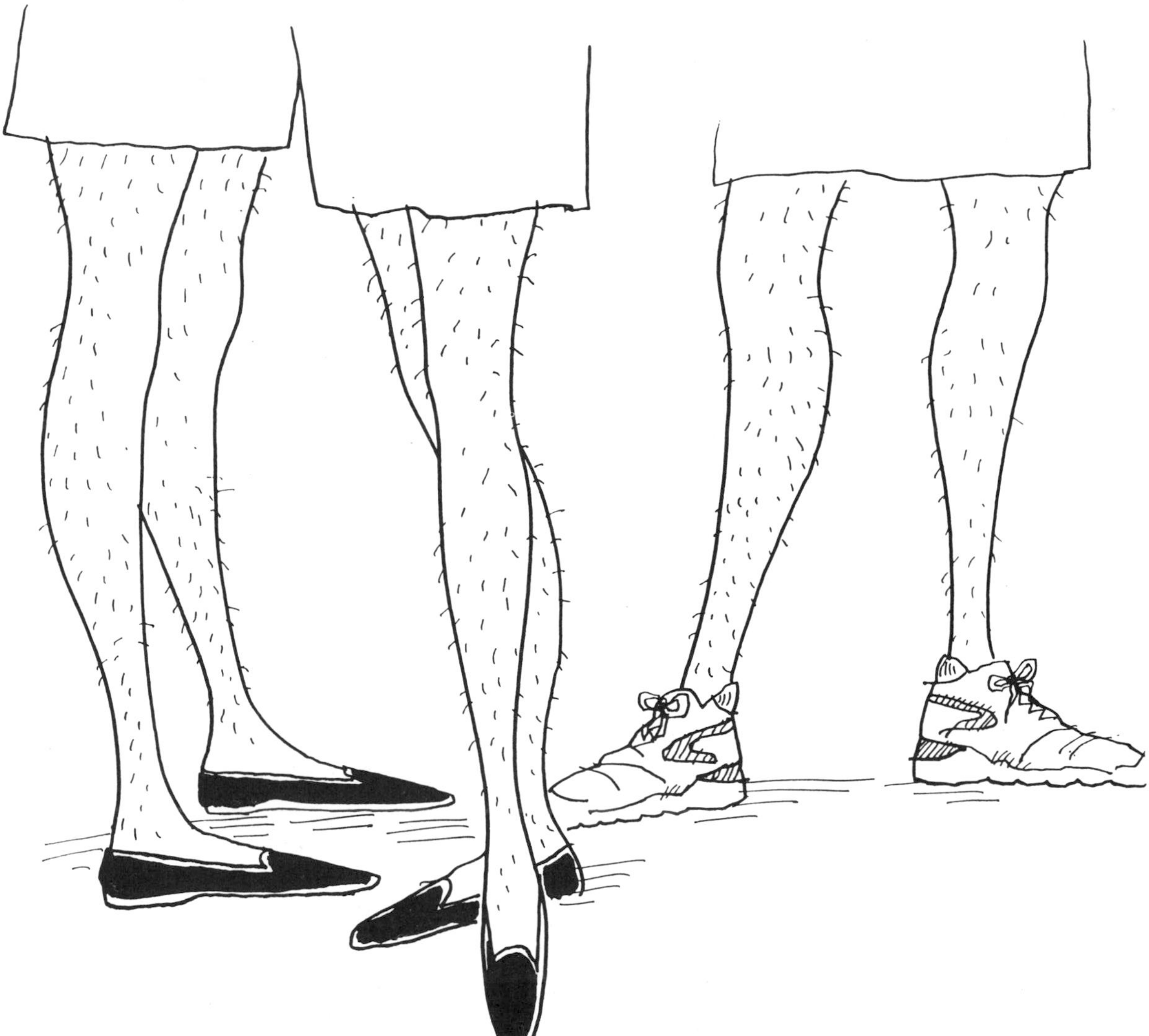

A WORLD WITHOUT WOMEN

HE

1) A marked increase in the sales of sweat clothes.
2) No more toilet-seat strife.
3) All sports, all the time.
4) The tuxedo becomes extinct.
5) No personal discussions about anything. Ever.

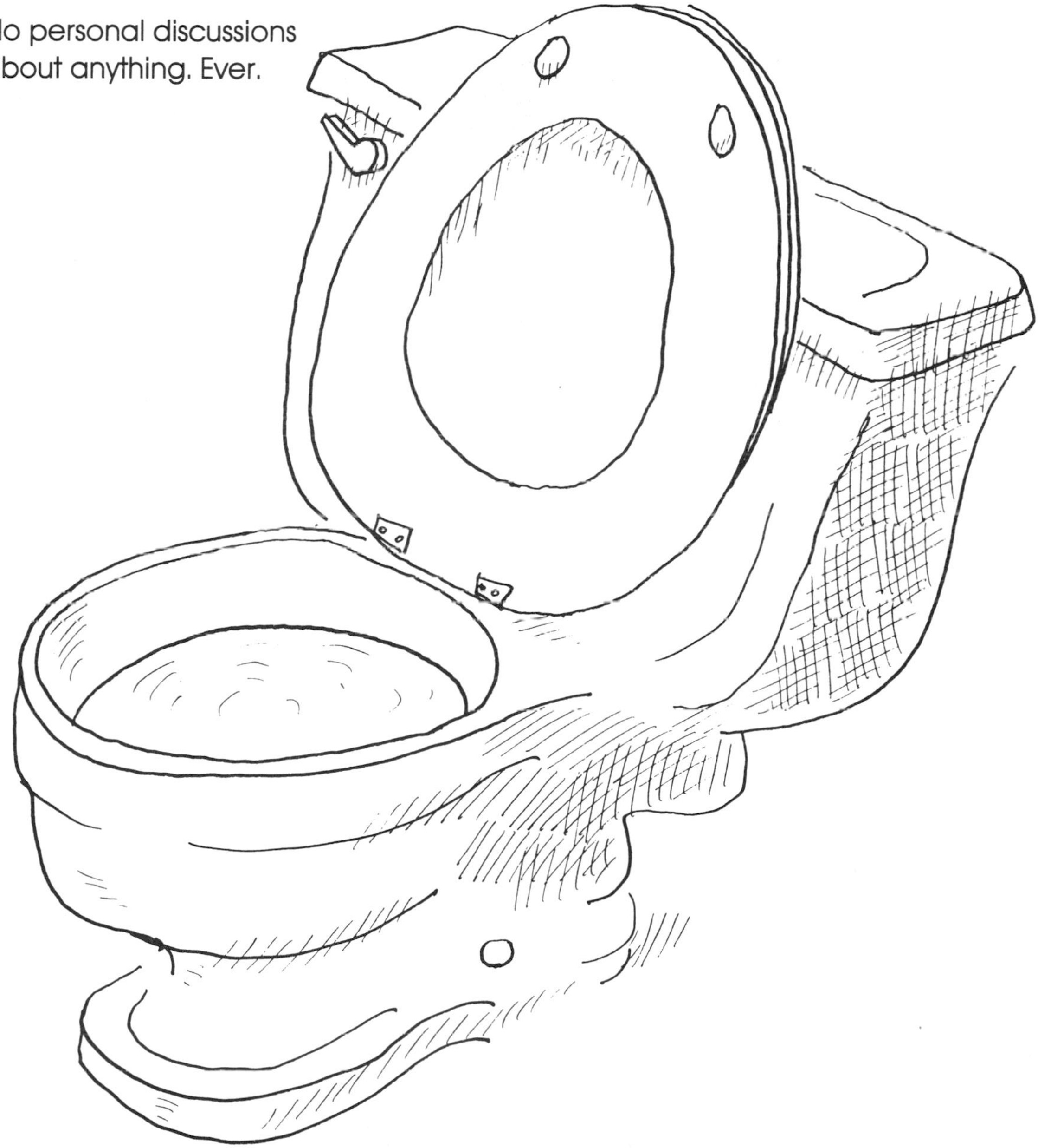